D0250290

This readable book gives sensible, warm-hearted advice to girls and their parents. It's written by expert clinicians who use state-of-the-art research and their own experiences with families to answer a wide range of important questions. This book will help the Ophelias of the 21st century and their parents. I recommend it.

— Dr. Mary Pipher, author of *Reviving Ophelia* and *The Middle of Everywhere*

The Inside Story on Teen Girls

305.235
Z18i

The Inside Story on Teen Girls

Experts Answer **Parents'** Questions

**Alice Rubenstein, EdD, and
Karen Zager, PhD**

Christian Heritage
College Library
2100 Greenfield Dr.
E Cajon. CA 92019

APA
LifeTools

American Psychological Association • Washington, DC

Copyright © 2002 by the American Psychological Association. All rights reserved. Except as permitted under the United States Copyright Act of 1976, no part of this publication may be reproduced or distributed in any form or by any means, or stored in a database or retrieval system, without the prior written permission of the publisher.

Published by
American Psychological Association
750 First Street, NE
Washington, DC 20002
www.apa.org

To order
APA Order Department
P.O. Box 92984
Washington, DC 20090-2984

Tel: (800) 374-2721, Direct: (202) 336-5510
Fax: (202) 336-5502, TDD/TTY: (202) 336-6123
On-line: www.apa.org/books/
E-mail: order@apa.org

In the U.K., Europe, Africa, and the Middle East, copies may be ordered from
American Psychological Association
3 Henrietta Street
Covent Garden, London
WC2E 8LU England

Typeset in Minion by EPS Group Inc., Easton, MD

Printer: Phoenix Color Corporation, Hagerstown, MD
Cover Designer: Naylor Design, Washington, DC
Technical/Production Editor: Jennifer L. Macomber

The opinions and statements published are the responsibility of the authors, and such opinions and statements do not necessarily represent the policies of the American Psychological Association.

Library of Congress Cataloging-in-Publication Data
Zager, Karen (Karen M.)
    The inside story on teen girls / by Karen Zager and Alice Rubenstein.—
1st ed.
        p. cm.
    ISBN 1-55798-892-7 (alk. paper)
    1. Teenage girls. 2. Adolescence. 3. Parent and teenager.
I. Rubenstein, Alice K. II. Title.

HQ798 .Z34 2002
305.235—dc21

2002020532

British Library Cataloguing-in-Publication Data
A CIP record is available from the British Library.

Printed in the United States of America
First Edition

To our significant others, Andy and Howard, for supporting us, loving us, and putting up with us during years of research and writing.

To our children, Heather, Jennifer, Erik, and Russell, for challenging us and keeping us truthful, honest, and humble.

To our mothers, Gertrude and Eleanor, who nurtured us through our own adolescence and who continue to love and guide us.

And to our fathers, Paul and Harold, who celebrated us as daughters and women and who remained young at heart throughout their lives.

We are so grateful to you all.—*Alice and Karen*

Feelings of worth can flourish only in an atmosphere where individual differences are appreciated, mistakes are tolerated, communication is open, and rules are flexible—the kind of atmosphere that is found in a nurturing family.

Virginia Satir

Contents

Acknowledgments

This book was a labor of love and would not have been "born" without the assistance and support of many friends and colleagues:

- Julia Frank-McNeil, our editor and Director of APA Books, who steadfastly believed in the project and provided unending help and encouragement throughout.
- Gary R. VandenBos, PhD, APA Publisher, who made the idea of this book a possibility and who stood by us every step of the way.
- Dr. Dorothy Cantor, APA Past President, for having the wisdom and foresight to convene a Task Force on Adolescent Girls and provide us with the forum from which this project emerged.
- Dr. Norine Johnson, Co-chair of the Task Force on Adolescent Girls and APA Past President, for her

friendship, insight, and commitment to recognizing and supporting the strengths and resiliency of adolescent girls.

- Dara Querimit, our graduate research assistant, who volunteered so generously of her time, energy, and ideas.

- Mary Campbell, APA Children, Youth, and Families Officer, who was a calming and reassuring anchor, as well as an invaluable source of information and coordination during the research phase of the project.

- Gabriele S. Clune, Manager of the Task Force on Adolescent Girls, who also provided staff support.

- Jessica Kohout, PhD, Director of the APA Research Office, who provided the research expertise for the data analysis.

- TOPSS (Teachers of Psychology in the Secondary Schools), who distributed the survey questions to adolescents and parents across the country and without whose help and support this book could never have been written.

- The hundreds of teens and parents who responded to our survey and asked us the questions that form the core of this book.

- The adolescents and their parents who have sought out our professional help, trusted us with their innermost thoughts and feelings, and from whom we have learned so very much. You have truly been our best teachers.

- And, of course, our deepest gratitude goes to our

panel of experts, who gave so generously of their time and contributed their psychological knowledge, perspective, and expertise. By providing us with their unique perspectives to the questions raised by hundreds of teens and their parents, they have ensured that this book reflects a diversity of experience and background and a breadth of psychological knowledge that can only come from having so many "coauthors." Our panel included

Carolyn Anderson, PhD, Rochester, NY
Noemi Balinth, PhD, New York, NY
Larry Beer, EdD, Kalamazoo, MI
Bonnie L. Blankmeyer, PhD, San Antonio, TX
Margaret Charlton, PhD, Aurora, CO
Priscilla Wilson Clancy, PhD, Dahlonega, GA
W. James Cosse, PhD, Hartsdale, NY
Donald K. Freedheim, PhD, Cleveland, OH
Bruce M. Gilberg, PhD, Rochester, NY
Sandra Haber, PhD, New York, NY
Norine G. Johnson, PhD, Boston, MA
Gerald P. Koocher, PhD, Boston, MA
John E. Northman, PhD, Buffalo, NY
Jackson Rainer, PhD, Boiling Springs, NC
Michael J. Salamon, PhD, Hewlett, NY
Marla M. Sanzone, PhD, Annapolis, MD
Michael Schwarzchild, PhD, Brookfield, CT
Peter L. Sheras, PhD, Charlottesville, VA
Ellen W. Williams, PhD, Tempe, AZ

About the Authors

Alice Rubenstein, EdD, is a psychologist in private practice in upstate New York and the mother of two terrific girls. She is founder and partner in the Monroe Psychotherapy and Consultation Center, where she provides individual, family, and relationship counseling. For the past 25 years, much of her work has focused on adolescents and parenting, including consultation with schools and community agencies that serve teens and their families. She is a core consultant to the U.S. Department of Health and Human Services Office of Adolescent Health and served as a consultant to the PBS documentary film *5 Girls*. She is frequently interviewed by the radio and print media, including *Newsweek*, *Shape*, *Self*, *Sassy*, and the new Health Scout Web site.

Dr. Rubenstein has served on the American Psychological Association (APA) Presidential Task Force on Adolescents Girls, as well as the Task Force on Women and Depression. As Director of the APA Division of Psychotherapy Brochure Project, she has spearheaded the development of a series of public information brochures that address issues of concern to both parents and professionals who work with teens. These include *Attention Deficit Disorder in Children and Adolescents* and *A Parent's Guide to Psychotherapy with Children and Adolescents*. She was chosen as the Distinguished Speaker by the APA Office of Continuing Education and is the author of numerous articles and book chapters on how to understand, communicate, and work with adolescents. She is the recipient of the Distinguished Psychologist Award from the Division of Psychotherapy of the APA and has served as President of the Division.

Karen Zager, PhD, is a psychologist in private practice in New York, specializing in adolescence, parenting, and relationship issues. She was featured in the MTV *Warning Signs* anti-violence video and consulted on the PBS documentary film *5 Girls*. She has been interviewed for dozens of magazines and newspapers, including *USA Today, The Washington Post, The Wall Street Journal, Ladies Home Journal, Parent Magazine, Cosmo Girl, Time,* and *Mademoiselle,* and is a regular contributor to *YM Magazine*. She has frequently been interviewed on TV (*Good Morning*

America, CBS Eyewitness News, Fox 5 News, *The O'Reilly Report*, *The Donohue Show*, and *Sally Jesse Raphael*), as well as on the radio and Web sites to discuss topics of adolescence and parenting. She was the recipient of the American Psychological Association (APA) Presidential Citation for contributions to the field of psychology and the Distinguished Psychologist of the Year Award from Psychologists in Independent Practice of the APA. She served as co-chair of the APA Presidential Task Force on Adolescent Girls and was President of Psychologists in Independent Practice, a Division of the APA. She is also a wife and the proud mother of two teenagers.

Introduction

Most parents would agree that raising an adolescent girl today can be very stressful. The joys of parenting are often masked by the struggles and challenges that you face. You chose this book because you are looking for something that directly addresses the kinds of questions and problems that you encounter every day. Here, you will find just what you have been looking for.

How This Book Came to Be Written

Several years ago, we had the opportunity to participate in an American Psychological Association Task Force on Adolescent Girls. It was during this time that we decided we wanted to write a book that would directly help teen girls and their parents, teachers, doctors, and other professionals who work with them.

However, even though as psychologists we have both worked with many, many adolescents and their parents, we did not want to write a book that was based only on our own experiences and perceptions. So, we decided to survey a much larger and more diverse group of adolescents, parents, teachers, and others who work with them to find out what they really want and need to know. We asked approximately 1,100 teens, parents, teachers, and other professionals the following question: "If you had the chance to have a private and confidential conversation with an expert with a great deal of knowledge and understanding about the concerns of adolescent girls today, what would you ask them? Please write down six questions about anything that is on your mind."

The teens, parents, and others we surveyed come from almost every racial, ethnic, and religious group in the country. Some of them live in cities, some in the suburbs, and others in small towns or in the countryside. They come from every income level. As a group, they asked us more than 6,000 questions. While we would have loved to answer every question, they would simply not all fit into this book! So, we chose those questions that were asked most often and seemed most important.

To our surprise, race, region, income, ethnic background, and religion did not seem to make much of a difference in the kinds of questions asked. It seems that parenting and working with adolescent girls presents us all with many of the same challenges. While the adolescent girls we surveyed represented a very diverse group, we found that teen girls from all over the country, as well as parents, teachers, and others who work with them, all have many of the same concerns.

As we thought about how to answer their questions, we realized that, as many of you can imagine, almost every question could have more than one answer. The answers might vary depending on the specific situation; the age, maturity, and personality of the teen; parenting style; and a family's religious, cultural, and ethnic background. And, as you already know, there is no single or simple answer to any question about raising or working with an adolescent girl! Therefore, it became very important to us to offer a broader perspective than that of just two experts.

So, we decided to bring together a panel of psychologists from all over the country, from diverse backgrounds and work settings. We asked each of our experts to give us their ideas about how they would answer the questions included in this book. As a result, the answers incorporate the very best thoughts, perspectives, and concrete suggestions of almost 50 psychologists with expertise in working with adolescent girls.

What Can I Do to Raise a Healthy Daughter?

The parents we surveyed asked this question over and over again, in many forms and with somewhat different wording, but the question was essentially the same. It is clear that as parents you want do everything you can for your daughter, but sometimes you just don't know what to do or how to do it.

Parents like you want to know what is "normal" for a teenage girl and what they should watch for that might mean that their daughter is in trouble. They want to know what rules and limits their daughter should have at what ages, when they are supposed to *let go*, and what they're supposed to *let go of*.

In a world that is changing more rapidly than most of us could have ever imagined, you want to know what you need to do to prepare your daughter for the future. You want to know how to keep her safe. But, at the same time, you want to support your daughter in going out into the world so she can gain the skills and confidence she needs to become a strong and resilient woman. You want to give your daughter the confidence to *reach for the stars!*

Raising a teenage girl is no easy task. As a parent, you want to give your daughter everything you can. But at times the challenges you come up against leave you feeling confused, lost, and sometimes frightened. You might even feel angry and hurt because your daughter does not seem to appreciate any of your efforts. But you don't give up. As hard and as frustrating as it gets, you are committed to doing whatever you can to help your daughter become a healthy, happy, fulfilled, and independent woman.

This book will help guide you through the complex maze of parenting an adolescent girl. Because there is such diversity among teens and their parents, there is simply no "one-size-fits-all" answer to any of the questions we were asked. There is more than one perspective and therefore more than one answer for almost every question. We hope that the multiple answers we have provided will help you make the choices that best fit your needs and situations.

This book will give you not only a greater understanding of your daughter's world, but tons of ideas and concrete suggestions about how to deal with all sorts of problems and concerns. Read it through— and then keep it nearby so you can use it as a reference when you need it!

And of course go ahead and sneak a look at the flip side of this book—find out what your daughter wants to know and what we are telling her about how to deal with all sorts of things, including you, her parents. And because we know your daughter won't be able to resist, we've invited her to check out this part of the book too!

The Inside Story on Teen Girls

1

Why Is She So Difficult to Deal With? Understanding and Communicating With Adolescent Girls

My daughter Emily is 15. Although we've lived in the same house all these years, you'd think we've come from totally different worlds. Most of the time it feels like we don't even speak the same language. Emily and I used to have wonderful heart-to-heart talks all the time. She would tell me everything; it was the kind of mother–daughter relationship I always dreamed of having.

But when Emily hit her teens, everything started to change. Slowly but surely she shut me out of her life. Now she doesn't tell me anything! It really hurts. No matter how hard I try, she says I just don't understand her, that I don't listen to her, and that I'm always criticizing her. Her moods are all over the map—one minute she's a sweetheart, the next minute it's like she's possessed by the devil! I wonder sometimes if she has any positive feelings about me or anyone in our family at all. Every time we try to talk, it winds up being a shouting match. We just can't seem to communicate about anything. It's so frustrating. I wish our relationship could go back to the way it used to be.

I love my daughter. I only want the best for her. I want her to be prepared for the challenges ahead of her. I want her to be able to take control of her own life. I want her to have the information she needs to develop healthy relationships. I want her to become a responsible, independent, and self-motivated woman.

But if Emily and I can't even talk about the things like her curfew or the clothes she wears, how can we talk about the really important things, like sex and drugs and friendships and romances and the future? Will our relationship ever go back to the way it was? Will we ever again have the closeness we used to have?—*Magda, mother of Emily, age 15*

I would like my daughter to articulate her feelings and share her ideas. How can I let her know that I am open to listening to her without judging her? *Katherine S.*

You are certainly not alone in wishing that your daughter would talk with you more about her feelings, thoughts, and ideas. While most adolescent girls will tell you that they'd certainly rather talk to their friends than their parents, don't think that this means you've been entirely replaced. The key to getting your daughter to share more with you is creating the kind of relationship and family atmosphere that makes it comfortable and inviting for your daughter to open up.

Here are some useful tips that will help your daughter see you as open to listening to her without being viewed as judgmental:

- *Watch your tone of voice.* Do you sound authoritarian, condescending, or patronizing? If you do, your daughter is likely to become indignant, distant, or turned off.
- *Listen.* Give your daughter acknowledgment, empathy, and support rather than your opinion about what she should do or how she should feel.
- *Be self-disclosing.* Tell your daughter how you may have felt similarly at her age or in similar circumstances.
- *Offer constructive suggestions.* Watch for the opportunity to offer input, but don't "teach" or "preach."

Watch for signs like the roll of her eyes or the

shrug of her shoulders to let you know that you and your daughter are not connecting. You don't need to act like her *friend* for your daughter to want to share her feelings and ideas with you. After all, you are her parent, and you can't pretend to be otherwise. But what you *do* need to do is spend time together, just being with each other. Spending time together gives you the opportunity to share thoughts and feelings when the mood arises (which is *not* all the time). After all, you can't expect that your daughter will always be in the mood to open up to you. These kinds of conversations often have to emerge spontaneously; they can't always be scheduled.

However, you can maximize your chances by creating "opportunities" to connect with your daughter:

- While you might feel like a taxi service, driving your daughter to and from activities is one of the best times to talk.
- Make a point of stopping by her room during the evening hours, when she's winding down and might want to chat.
- Plan on a breakfast or lunch for just the two of you, once a month, and let her decide where to go.

Remember, the more often you are available, the more likely it is that your daughter will share her feelings and ideas with you.

* * *

During her teen years, your daughter is supposed to start to develop values, opinions, and beliefs of her own. Typically, teens "clam up" because they are trying to be independent and develop their own separate identities. Teenagers are often more likely to share their thoughts with their peers than with their parents, because they anticipate that their parents will be judgmental, disapproving, and possibly very controlling. They assume, often correctly, that their peers will agree with them and their parents won't! So it's frequently difficult to create an atmosphere in which your daughter feels free to express her feelings and share her ideas with you.

One of the mistakes that many parents make is that they approach their daughters with the expectation that a "talk" has to be lengthy, serious, and obviously "meaningful" to count. Discard those expectations entirely. Some of the best talks happen in quick snippets that last only a minute or two. They might be short, but they have a big impact. A talk might occur between phone calls, on the way in or out of the shower, or when you are serving as your daughter's chauffeur. Just because these conversations aren't "sit down and let's really connect" type of talks doesn't mean that your daughter isn't sharing some of her innermost thoughts and feelings with you.

Another mistake made by many parents is that they ask the wrong questions. Questions like "Why don't you talk to me about your life any more?" or "Do you know how bad I feel that you never tell me anything?" might make your daughter feel guilty enough to throw you a crumb, but they will never get you a decent piece of the pie! These types of questions are experienced as far too demanding, intrusive, and controlling. So, eliminate them totally from your repertoire.

Don't try to make your daughter feel guilty: It doesn't work. And don't make a habit of talking to her repeatedly about things that she would regard as unpleasant: rules, curfew, school grades, and chores. Instead, pay attention to the things that are going on in your daughter's life, and use those as a springboard to connect with her. Ask her simple questions about what she was doing, whether she enjoyed it, who she was with, and what her plans are. Let the conversation flow from there.

And one final note: If you want your daughter to talk with you, go to where *she* is, don't ask her to come to where you are. Stop by her room, be willing to hang out with her while she's getting ready to go out, or even stay up late to touch base with her when she returns home from being with her friends. You might only get a "Hi," or you might actually get a "taste of the pie"!

Does a teenage girl have to rebel? Can it be prevented, or is it unavoidable? Does there have to be friction between adolescent girls and their parents?
Michelle P.

It's a myth that teen girls must fight with their parents for them to have a successful passage into adulthood. While popular culture depicts and high-lights a great deal of turmoil between teen girls and their parents, particularly their mothers, extreme re-bellion is rare. So, try not to label your daughter's healthy push to have a *reasonable* degree of indepen-dence as "rebelling."

It is your job to gradually increase your daughter's freedoms and responsibilities so that by the time she is ready to go off on her own (either to college or to work), she is able to protect herself, manage her money and time, and pick good friends. By gradually increasing her independence, your daughter is not only less likely to rebel but also more likely to turn to you later on for guidance and advice. If you do not allow your daughter to develop her independence, she is much more likely to resort to rebellion to separate and grow.

* * *

As they get older, teenagers need to feel an in-creasing degree of control over their life choices. As they seek to gain more control, you lose control. Some parents find it difficult to accept that they must "let go" and describe their daughters as "rebellious" when in fact their daughters are simply growing up! While the vast majority of teens go through a normal period of rebellion as part of establishing their own separate identities, there are some teens whose behav-iors are so extreme that the rebellion cannot be con-sidered healthy or normal. In these extreme cases, pro-fessional help is needed. But for most teens, rebellion is natural, normal, and healthy. You might not like it, but you have to accept it. Your daughter is developing her own identity—separate from the family.

One of the things you can do to minimize the amount of conflict between you and your daughter is to take a close look at your parenting style and change your approach if it is too extreme. On the one hand, excessive or seemingly arbitrary, authoritarian control can contribute to extreme rebellion by too severely limiting your daughter's opportunity for self-expression and exploration of her self and her world. It may create a "forbidden-fruit" phenomenon, whereby your daughter rebels to get a taste of everything that has been so austerely limited.

On the other hand, parents who think they can avoid conflict and rebellion by being overly permissive and "laissez-faire" inadvertently create a different problem, because not only do teens need structure and limits to stay safe, but they need to have some limits to rebel against! In other words, if you provide insufficient structure, discipline, or authority, your daughter may rebel more severely to get you to give her the structure and limits she needs. Although your daughter will probably balk at your rules, she needs them; so, set the rules, but also expect her to rebel. An unstructured or overly permissive household will not provide your daughter with a good model of impulse control or self-discipline. In fact, it will make it much more difficult for her to learn how to manage her urges, drives, and desires for self-gratification. In the end, parents who provide too little structure or discipline increase the chances of their daughters engaging in dangerous forms of rebellion.

Here are a few parenting tips that can help you create an environment that will help to prepare your daughter for greater independence, without pushing her to act out or rebel in extreme ways:

- *Communicate with your daughter.* Don't make the mistake of thinking that she needs to talk with you *less* as she becomes more independent. She needs to talk with you *more.*
- *Set reasonable limits.* If you don't know what kind of rules your daughter should have at any specific age, talk with other parents, her guidance counselor, or other professionals who are experts in adolescent development.
- *Provide predictable expectations and consequences.*
- *Discipline with respect.* Don't be hurtful. The purpose of discipline is to teach your daughter that there are consequences for inappropriate behavior or breaking the rules. Try to make the "punishment fit the crime." Don't go overboard.
- *Wait until you "cool down."* If you are looking for a way to "hurt" your daughter or get revenge, you are too angry to decide on a consequence just yet.

But remember, you do *not* have total control over whether or not your daughter will rebel in a negative way. And parenting style does not totally predict which teens will rebel and to what degree. Environment, your daughter's temperament, and peer relationships and pressures are all important factors in determining how your daughter will behave as she seeks greater independence and autonomy.

* * *

Some adolescent girls, particularly those who have older brothers, often complain that they are not allowed the same "freedoms" that their brothers or male peers are given. While there are certainly some situations in which girls are more at risk than boys, be careful not to impose your own bias or stereotypes on your daughter just because she is a girl.

Gender stereotypes can contribute to friction between teenage girls and their parents. Take a minute to think about your own stereotypes and expectations of girls versus boys. Do you think boys should be more independent than girls? Do you think they should be stronger or tougher? Do you think boys should have more freedoms? Do you ultimately believe that boys are more likely to be successful than girls? Your daughter can come to believe that your stereotyped view of girls applies directly to her, and this can result in low self-esteem, a lack of self-confidence, and the perception of herself as less competent and able than she really is. Or, your daughter might react by refusing to accept your views, and in the process of rebelling against them, she might reject even reasonable and appropriate concerns that you may have about her safety and security. If your daughter feels that you are arbitrarily restricting her or that you do not see her as a capable person simply because she is female, she will either come to expect less of herself or rebel against you. And even worse than living through the rebellion is the long-term damage these kinds of stereotypes can cause.

Parents can help minimize friction between themselves and their daughters by starting early to empower their daughters to identify their physical, emotional, social, and intellectual strengths. Adolescent girls who are given freedom and independence on the basis of their real ability, and not restricted simply because they are girls, are less likely to act out and rebel against their parents. And they are much more likely to develop a strong sense of self-worth, self-confidence, and good judgment.

How can I respond to and help my daughter with her mood swings?
Jasmine W.

It's a fact: Mood swings in teen girls are normal. At the same time, it would probably be hard to find a parent who wouldn't agree that their daughter's mood swings sometimes drive them crazy! At times, it can seem like your daughter goes from elated to miserable in a split second, three or four times a day! The challenge is to find that delicate balance between acknowledging the intensity of your daughter's feelings while keeping sight of the fact that mood swings are normal.

Encourage your daughter to verbalize her thoughts and feelings to you. Let her know that you understand what she is going through and how difficult it is. Remind her that while you are now her parent, you were once a teenager and you remember what a difficult time it was. It is important to remind yourself, and sometimes your daughter, that mood swings at this time are natural and normal, and they will pass.

Help her learn appropriate ways of dealing with her emotions. Work with her to find stress-relieving activities for those really rough times. Point out to her that physical activity, exercise, sports, or even just taking a walk can sometimes help a lot. But don't try to do this kind of problem solving when your daughter is smack in the middle of one of her tough times. Instead, look for a calm period to discuss these issues. Periods of instability are not the most likely times to be able to carry on a reasonable conversation. Let her know that you understand how she feels and that you hurt when she hurts.

Even if you try your very best and do everything right, your daughter may still be unbearably moody and snap your head off every time you try to communicate with her. There are simply those times when your goodwill and patience are just not enough. The best way to handle this is to try not to react. Don't fight fire with fire. Don't get caught up in arguing about her moodiness. For example, if you ask her a question, and she responds in a rather nasty tone "Just leave me alone!", don't get into a debate about her tone of voice. Just let it go (in spite of your desire to snap her head off).

* * *

Adolescent girls experience mood swings for many different reasons. Talking to your daughter will allow you to better understand some of the stresses that are contributing to her mood swings. Help your daughter to identify ways in which she can reduce those stresses. For example, you might try teaching her some relaxation techniques, give her a journal in which she can express her feelings in writing or drawing, or encourage her to get involved in a physical activity (like dance, karate, kick-boxing). The most important thing is to let your daughter know that you care about her feelings and that you are available to listen and help her problem solve.

* * *

Mood swings occur with different intensity, frequency, and duration in different girls. So, you need to think about how intense your daughter's mood swings are, how frequently they happen, and how long they last. It is not necessary to be overly concerned with mild and occasional mood swings. Not every occurrence of a mood swing requires professional attention.

If your daughter's mood swings are only mild, you can try to help her identify and express her feelings before they build up and become a big problem. But if her mood swings are frequent, intense, persistent, or detrimental to her social or academic life, you may want to seek a professional opinion. Generally, if your daughter's mood swings create social or academic problems, or if they are causing your daughter to harm herself or others, she needs professional attention.

If your daughter's mood swings result in inappropriate behavior that is really hurtful or disrespectful, you need to clearly state that such behavior will not be tolerated. You can accept all of her feelings but not necessarily all of the ways she behaves when she expresses them. While there should be consequences for inappropriate behavior, there should not be negative consequences for her expressing her feelings, even if you think she's being unreasonably moody.

Why does my adolescent daughter want to be distant from the family? *Victoria M.*

While it's easy and probably accurate to say that your daughter seems to stay distant from the family, has it occurred to you that there are many times when you secretly wish that the distance were even greater? It might help you to know that many parents have found themselves whispering under their breath "I just need a break. A *long* break."

On a more serious note, it's one of those painful ironies of life that just when your adolescent daughter is mature enough to relate to you as a person and perhaps as a friend, she pulls away. Try to remember that this pulling away is a natural expression of her maturation; don't take it personally. Your daughter's primary focus right now is her peers. Most often, it's not that she doesn't want to be with her family, it's that she wants to be with her friends.

Try setting aside designated "family times" that are fun for everyone. Emphasize to your daughter that you enjoy her company and want to spend time with her. Don't complain that she is spending too much time with her friends. Instead, suggest that she invite her friends over to your house. Show positive interest in your daughter's friends and try to get to know them as people. There is usually one home in the neighborhood where the kids tend to congregate. The parents are usually pleasant, in a good mood, and genuinely enjoy having the kids around. This home usually has a space where the teens can have some privacy. It's the kind of place where the parents don't insist that every area of the house is perfectly neat at all times.

If your daughter and her friends see your home as an inviting hangout, and you are watchful but not overly intrusive, she'll bring her friends over more often, and you will feel less distant because you will be more connected to an important part of her life. The parent–child relationship is in a process of change during the teen years. If you work to recognize, accept, and adapt to these changes, your relationship with your daughter will grow into one that is mutually rewarding.

* * *

Adolescence is a time of learning about the world and gaining independence and autonomy. We know from research and through common sense that adolescents do prefer to have more time on their own, away from their parents, to learn about the world, to make new friends, and to learn about themselves as independent and autonomous individuals. There is always a pull between an adolescent's need to be secure and dependent and her need to be autonomous and independent. Parents need to be understanding and accepting when their daughter asks for private time and space. Parents who support their daughter's requests for private time and space are also more likely to get her to be willing to spend some quality time as a family.

However, if your daughter has become so distant from you and the family that you feel there is no connection at all, take a look at the kinds of activities you are trying to get her to join in on. Do these activities reflect any of her interests? Does she get the opportunity to make suggestions about how the family will spend time together? If you make family activities appealing to her, at least some of the time, she is more likely to want to join in.

How do I keep our conversations from becoming shouting matches? How do I keep the communication lines open?
Brian G.

During their teen years, adolescent girls are developing their own ideas and exercising thought processes they never had as children, and they are often quite passionate in their expression of these thoughts. As frustrating as it is at times, it is easier to help your daughter to calm down and lower her voice than to get an uncommunicative teen to talk about her feelings. Remember, you want your daughter to talk about her thoughts and feelings. You just want her to do it in a respectful and appropriate manner. As the adult, you have to set the example and be willing to take responsibility for your own behavior. If you raise your voice and yell when you are angry, then you are modeling this behavior for your daughter.

The first rule in trying not to get into a shouting match with your daughter is to listen. Listening doesn't mean you agree. And don't tell your daughter that she is "wrong." This is a surefire way to shut down the lines of communication in a hurry. Respect your daughter's opinions and ideas. If you want her to feel comfortable talking with you about her thoughts and feelings, she must feel she can express herself without being judged. Keep the discussion focused on the issues at hand as much as possible, and choose your battles. Many things are simply not worth fighting over. Sometimes parents just want control, and they don't discriminate between the important and unimportant issues.

If you look to maintain the same control over your daughter now as you did when she was a child, you can forget about her ever being willing to communicate with you. Remember that you want your daughter to grow into a mature, independent young woman who can use her mind and express her thoughts and feelings effectively. Set the example and let her know that even though you may have differing views, you are always willing to listen and respect her right to disagree with you. Although in the end you may insist on having the final say, the time and patience you invest in talking with your daughter will pay off.

* * *

To keep the lines of communication open, parents need to understand what they are feeling and be able to convey their feelings directly to their daughters. For instance, when your daughter comes in too late at night, you can say, "I was worried that you got into an accident" or "I care about you. That's why I was very concerned that you came home much later than you had promised to. I was afraid that you were stuck somewhere and needed help." Judgmental comments like "Where have you been? You are grounded" will typically elicit an angry response and rarely elicit anything resembling open communication. This is exactly the kind of situation that can easily result in a shouting match. You raise your voice; she raises her voice. Neither of you are really listening to the other, and no one's feelings are being heard or respected.

Instead of jumping into anger, look inside yourself to see if what you are really feeling is worry, sadness, or hurt. If that's what the core feeling is, express it honestly. State the positive feelings first: that you care, you love her, and you would like to be helpful. If you do this, your daughter is likely to feel less defensive and more willing to talk with you.

When you do have to set rules, be nonjudgmental. Don't be a historian and criticize your daughter for everything she has done wrong in the past year, and don't get carried away with accusations. Clearly state the expectations, rules, and penalties for breaking the rules in advance. Don't waver. But also be sure to praise your daughter directly and frequently when she does something correctly and behaves appropriately. For instance, "I really appreciated that you called the other day when you were stuck at the library because of the rain. I would have been very worried if I didn't hear from you. It made me feel reassured and more trusting." In other words, be sure to give her credit whenever she deserves it.

Is it normal for my 14-year-old daughter to be angry at me sometimes? *Carrie B.*

Like love, anger is a very passionate feeling. Take a moment to think about this question: Is there anyone you really love whom you've never been angry at? If you are honest with yourself, your answer will be "no."

Anger is the emotion we sometimes feel when others do not give us what we want, need, or think we deserve. We may react with anger when we feel unappreciated, misunderstood, and misjudged or when "life just isn't fair." Anger is a normal feeling that everyone has at some time, including 14-year-old daughters.

You can't avoid your daughter's anger all the time, because you cannot *always* be appreciative, understanding, and giving. It is normal for your daughter to have angry feelings. It is important for you to accept her feelings, including her anger, and to allow the appropriate expression of her angry feelings. Some examples of the appropriate expression of anger include statements such as "I'm so angry at you. You are so unfair. I don't want to talk to you at all!" or "I don't care what you have to say, I'm not listening to you now." Some families will even allow yelling, screaming, and cursing as ways to express anger—it is up to you where you draw the line. However, what is definitely over the line and unacceptable is physical abuse, verbal abuse, hurting anyone, or damaging property. But don't forget, the same rules for how anger can be expressed should apply to every member of the family.

Remember, if you don't allow your daughter to express her anger (or other feelings, for that matter), she may wind up with more serious problems. Children who do not learn how to express their feelings can't learn how to cope with them. Your daughter may have difficulty later on in life if she does not learn how to appropriately deal with her negative or upset feelings.

* * *

Everyone gets angry sometimes! Your daughter may be angry at you because, among other reasons, she does not understand why she has to follow the rules you may have set, why she cannot stay out late, or why she has to make schoolwork such a priority. While your rules and expectations may seem totally appropriate and fair to you, your daughter is likely to see some or all of your rules as too strict. Even though you may try to explain the reasons for your rules, teenagers often have difficulty seeing another person's point of view when it does not agree with their own. So, while you may insist that your daughter obey the rules, you cannot insist on her agreeing with them or not being angry at you.

It is really crucial that you understand how truly difficult it can be for your daughter to see and understand your point of view. It seems so simple on the surface, but in fact, it is a difficult developmental struggle to be able to put aside one's own way of looking at something and consider a whole different point of view. Many adults never develop this ability! These are the kinds of adults you've met at times—the ones who are annoying because they always need to be right. Your job as a parent is to help your daughter through this struggle until she gets to the point of maturity where she can see another person's viewpoint.

Meanwhile, as a parent, you have both the right and the responsibility to set limits on your daughter's actions or behaviors. But no one, not even you as her parent, has the right to try to control your daughter's feelings. Unlike certain behaviors, feelings are never right or wrong—they are not subject to anyone's judgment. While you may not understand why your daughter is angry, you must accept her right to feel angry.

Why do teen girls insist they know more than their moms? *Grace A.*

First of all, as difficult as it may be to admit, there are times when daughters *do* know more than their moms. For example, do you remember how to factor a binomial equation? Can you rattle off the names of the elements in the periodic table? How about the economic causes of the Civil War? Do you ever rely on your teenager to help you out with the computer? The average teenage girl could probably run circles around her parents when it comes to technology. Many adults are still in the "dark ages" when it comes to using a computer to accomplish everyday life tasks, such as shopping on-line, ordering a pizza, or locating a book in the library. But for your daughter, it's no

24

big deal. So, sometimes your daughter insists that she knows more than her mother because she really *does* know more than her mother!

While parents certainly have the benefit of the wisdom that only experience can bring, it's a mistake to think that your daughter's world is the same as the one you grew up in. Teenagers today have access to much more information and are exposed to a far greater range of experiences than their parents were. So, for parents to think that they always know more than their kids is not only inaccurate but is likely to set the stage for oppositional and rebellious behaviors. Your daughter is more likely to listen to you, and consider your wisdom, if you are also willing to admit that there are things you don't know.

Second, part of being an adolescent includes the feeling of being invincible. Insisting that she knows more than you is just part of your daughter's normal feeling of invincibility. And because teenagers have learned an enormous amount (academically and socially) in a relatively short time, it is easy for them to feel like they know everything.

However, you as a parent have obviously had more life experiences, and you want your daughter to benefit from what your experiences have taught you. You certainly don't want your daughter to make the same mistakes that you did! Although it can be useful to share your experiences with your daughter, be careful not to talk about them in a way that sounds preachy or judgmental. Even though, at times, your daughter may not seem to be absorbing what you are trying to share with her, she is probably taking in more than you realize. And when the mood is right, your daughter might even be willing and eager to hear what you have to say.

It's not a contest of who knows more; it's just that you need to recognize that you and your daughter know different things.

* * *

For starters, teenage daughters insist they know more than their mothers because they need to! It is an important part of the process of figuring out who they are and who they are becoming. Whereas a child looks to her parents primarily as her caretakers and protectors and does not question everything, an adolescent is likely to question almost everything a parent says or does. For a teenage girl, being "not like Mom" is the initial reference point in her struggle to be her own person. It is very important to your teenage daughter that you begin to see her as a person with her own ideas and not just as "your daughter."

As with any other developmental change, this one is often not an easy or smooth process at first, and it can cause significant upheaval in your relationship. Often a parent can be caught off guard by this shift in the relationship, and it can feel like you can no longer do or say anything right. It really helps to remember that your daughter's newly discovered "knowing" is a healthy sign of her growing up. Try not to take it personally or as an indication that you are doing something wrong. If you are not defensive about your daughter's need to know more than you, it will be easier for you to validate for her that her views and ideas matter, even if you disagree with them.

For some parents, realizing that they no longer know everything is very difficult. It can feel like they are no longer an important resource. But the truth is that you have become a resource in a different way and for different things. Now what your daughter needs to know from you has changed. Knowing is no longer primarily gathering facts and information; it is about learning life skills, such as relating, compromising, negotiating, being assertive, problem solving, and planning for the future. So, celebrate the fact that your daughter "knows" more than you in some areas, and focus on teaching her the other more complicated life skills.

What can I say when my adolescent daughter has experienced failure and is upset? *Savannah H.*

Parents hurt when their kids hurt. A failure is not only painful for your daughter but is painful for you, too. This is one of those times when you wish you could make it all better, but you may not be able to. You can't make the pain disappear, but you can help your daughter to understand that failure is a normal, acceptable, and often unavoidable, experience throughout life.

Communicate to your daughter that failures are learning experiences and rarely lead to catastrophe. The beginning phases of helping your daughter face failure will involve a lot of listening and gently asking questions. Ask the kind of questions that will help you understand your daughter's feelings and the nature of the problem. Always begin with questions that can help your daughter clarify her feelings. Remember, your daughter is upset and needs a strong dose of empathy before she can be emotionally prepared for perspective taking and possible problem solving. Don't spout off about past failures, don't lecture, and don't make threats. At this point, you want to convey the message that although failures create temporary conditions of unhappiness, they are almost always filled with opportunities to learn.

Once your daughter has calmed down, she is ready for the next step. Help her to evaluate what, if anything, she can do *now*, either to improve the situation or to help to prevent it from happening again. This kind of problem solving should focus on specific actions she can take to help her to begin to feel some degree of control. For example, if your daughter tried out for one of the varsity sports and failed to make the team, she might look at other ways to belong to the team, like volunteering as scorekeeper or assistant manager. She might decide to join an intramural or club team, where she can continue to compete on a less intensive level. Or she might look for a team to join outside of school where she can work to improve her skills, with the goal of trying out for the varsity team again next year.

Sometimes your daughter might simply not be open to any of your suggestions or ideas. In fact, she might just want to wallow in her misery for a while! If she tells you something like "Don't tell me to cheer up, you don't know what you are talking about!", listen to her. Back off, get out of the way, and wait until she's ready to talk. Be patient. And don't assume that when she is ready to talk, she is going to talk to you. She may call a friend, talk to a brother or sister, or seek out another adult she trusts. Don't be offended. Remind yourself that the priority is solving the problem, not making you feel wanted or included.

Also keep in mind that, while you may be very tempted to solve your daughter's problems *for her*, it is best to have her take the lead, with you serving as a sounding board and a source of support and help if she needs it.

* * *

When your adolescent daughter has experienced failure and is upset, you need to offer her an attentive ear and unconditional support. Adolescents typically feel a strong sense of new capabilities and invincibility, so even small failures can be very upsetting. For instance, your daughter may have had an unrealistic expectation of herself in a particular situation. You can help your daughter figure out what she expected of herself and evaluate whether or not her expectations were realistic. If you find out that her expectations were not realistic, help her determine what she *should* expect of herself.

You can help your daughter make her goals more doable by breaking them down into smaller steps, so she can consistently feel competent by fulfilling her smaller, short-term goals. Encourage her to evaluate her successes: "Let's see what you have done well." Highlight her smaller successes and achievements. Remind her that each step is a building block toward her goal. Explain to her that some failures in life are small, but necessary, steps to bigger achievements.

Share your own experiences of failure with your daughter, and tell her how you dealt with them effectively. Sharing your experiences can not only be extremely helpful and reassuring to your daughter but can also help you to maintain your perspective by reflecting on your own teen years. You may also tell your daughter stories of famous and respected people who had experienced early failures in life. All of this will help your daughter to see how common failures are and how often they are part of the path to success. What is most important is to help your daughter maintain her positive self-esteem when she does not succeed.

* * *

As parents, we are used to trying to protect our children and to "fix" things that are wrong in their lives, to make things "all better" for them if we can. While younger children may need our protection and intervention, adolescents often need us just to listen

30

and understand how they feel. Teenage girls often have very big feelings "in the moment" and, at the time, their experiences of failure can feel heartbreaking and never-ending to them. While it is natural for you to want to make your daughter feel better, be careful that you don't wind up minimizing or trivializing her very deep feelings. Listen to your daughter, let her vent her feelings, and trust that at some point she will come to feel better. Remember, your daughter is not going to want to hear your advice until she has finished expressing her hurt and pain. The most important thing you can give your daughter at these times of "failure" is reassurance of your love and pride in her. Your advice is only secondary.

How much sexual knowledge is too much? Too little? *Chloe N.*

There is little disagreement that because of the increased risk of sexually transmitted diseases (STDs), such as AIDS, access to accurate information about sex is essential for adolescent girls. But, for many parents, talking about sex with their daughters can feel awkward, embarrassing, and uncomfortable. If your parents never talked with you about sex, you probably are not quite sure exactly how to approach the topic. And you might not have a clear idea of what your daughter already knows and doesn't know. It is *essential* that you overcome your hesitation, discomfort, or even fear, and *talk* to your daughter. It could save her life.

31

The bottom line is that it is very important that your daughter has access to accurate information about sex as soon as she is ready to learn about it. But how do you know what your daughter does and does not need to know at different stages of her development? And how do you know what information she is ready for? Generally speaking, once your daughter reaches her early teens, she should know all about her own body, including

- breast development
- underarm hair
- pubic hair
- pimples and acne
- getting her period and how to use a pad or tampon
- what she can do for cramps and PMS.

Your daughter should know where she can get information about sex, pregnancy, and STDs. She needs to know about yeast infections, urinary tract infections, and minor vaginal irritations. You are one source of that information, but this is also a good time to give your daughter one or two books that she can read privately, in case there are any questions that she does not feel comfortable asking you.

As she approaches menstruation and you begin to talk with her about it, you will have a good opportunity to discuss all of the changes that will be happening to her body and how these changes are a celebration of her developing into a woman. At the same time, your daughter needs to know that with these changes comes increased responsibility for taking charge of her own health and safety.

Often teens feel uncomfortable or embarrassed when their parents try to start a conversation about sex. But, as her parent, you need to overcome any of your own hesitation or embarrassment and take the lead in opening up the discussion. Regardless of your daughter's response, or your own reluctance, it is very important to provide her with as much information as possible. Many more adolescents get into trouble because of *lack* of information than *too much* information. If you do try to provide too much information before your daughter is ready, chances are that she will just tune you out, so no damage will be done. Listen carefully to the questions your daughter asks. And listen for those questions that may not be asked directly but that your daughter is just hinting about. In general, it is better to tell your daughter too much rather than too little.

* * *

A teen can't get "too much sexual knowledge," because acquiring accurate knowledge and understanding helps to provide a sense of safety and to calm fears or apprehensions. Providing your daughter with little or no information about sex leaves it all up to chance—she will get information from someone, but the information may be wrong or inaccurate. And you will have conveyed the message that you're not approachable to talk to about one of the most important issues in her life. It is far, far better to speak to your daughter openly about sex.

If you feel awkward or uncomfortable, practice: Ask a friend or your spouse or partner to listen to how you would introduce topics and some of the things you would talk about. If you can't find someone to listen to your talk, use a tape recorder and play it back for yourself. Saying these things out loud just once will put you much more at ease. You probably need to do some reading yourself, as there is now a great deal more information available. There are many more risks and many additional ways your daughter can protect herself against unwanted pregnancy and disease than when you were a teen.

Talk with your daughter about how sexuality is a powerful life force. Talk with her about the important choices she will have to make about sex. You can use this conversation as a springboard to discuss the related issues of self-esteem, peer pressure, and responsibility. And don't just talk about sex once. You need to keep bringing it up so that you can work toward having an open and ongoing dialogue over the course of your daughter's teen years.

* * *

You have to make a distinction between sexual knowledge and sexual activity. Your daughter can't have too much sexual knowledge, but she certainly can have too much sexual activity! In spite of all the media hype that promotes the message that girls and women can be as casual about sex as boys and men, without significant emotional consequences, this is just not true. In the vast majority of cases, girls struggle more with their feelings of having been sexually active than guys do. While there are several theories about why this is true, the fact is that your daughter needs to know that early sexual activity can be damaging to her self-esteem as well as her reputation. So as a parent, be sure to give her the message that having sexual knowledge in no way means she is ready for sexual activity.

As a parent, how can I effectively walk the tightrope between too little control and too much control? *Natalie R.*

For most parents, the issue of control during adolescence has to do with which decisions their teen makes and which decisions they still make. Typically, these struggles for control are about things like curfew, spending money, driving, hanging out with friends, whether your daughter is allowed to be at an unsupervised party, allowed to have her boyfriend over when no adult is home, or allowed to get rides with people you don't know. So, issues of control can arise in many different circumstances, and parents are often faced with trying to walk the tightrope between maintaining or giving up control.

While you want your daughter to have the experiences she needs to become a competent and resilient woman, you know that giving her too much to handle too soon can be harmful and maybe even disastrous. As your daughter enters her teen years, your role as her parent begins to change quite significantly. During her childhood, effective parenting involved setting clear, consistent limits. During adolescence, parenting evolves to include teaching your daughter how to effectively negotiate and compromise. Consistency and control still remain important, especially in regard to potential dangers, but they alone are not enough. Here is where negotiating and compromise come into the picture. It is your daughter's "job" to push the limits you set, and it is your "job" to slowly but surely teach your daughter how to negotiate and compromise to gain more and more freedom.

The teen years are a critically important time to teach your daughter these skills. As a young teen, your daughter's negotiating skills are equivalent to using a bludgeon or a baseball bat to beat the opposition into submission. But gradually, her skills should become more refined. It is through the push-pull over the rules and limits that your daughter will learn the important life skills of negotiating and compromising. By the end of her adolescence, your daughter should be able to voice her opinion, listen to what the other person thinks or wants, stand up for her own rights, and be able to negotiate acceptable compromises. These skills are developed through practice in interacting with parents, so you should plan on gradually giving up control. Instead, give more control to your daughter as she learns how to negotiate and compromise effectively.

* * *

As a parent, you probably exercised a considerable amount of control over your daughter until ages 11 or 12. But now your control must gradually ease up as your daughter has newfound intellectual, social, and emotional competencies. It is now time for you to begin to replace unilateral decision making and control with discussion and compromise.

The more you support your daughter's natural search for freedom and independence, and the more control is appropriately replaced by negotiation, the more you will learn about things such as a party, school activity, date, or concert. The goal is to assert control only when you believe a situation is unsafe or when the behavior is likely to have serious negative consequences for your daughter's future. When you do assert control, it *must* be enforceable. If you give your daughter a curfew, you need to be home at curfew time to make sure she has abided by the limit you have set. If you go away for the weekend and you do not want your daughter to have a party at the house, have her stay elsewhere, or have another adult stay in the house to house-sit. Don't be fooled into thinking that threats, promises, extra rewards, or bribes will give you control. You must *actively* take control of a situation if you feel it is potentially not safe or your daughter is not capable of managing on her own.

As your daughter matures and you let go of some control and loosen the limits, you must remain flexible. A rule that you may have set during her early teen years may become obsolete during her middle teens. And in her late teens, there may be almost no rules at all. Remember, this is a process, and you must allow your daughter to make and learn from her mistakes. So, don't automatically tighten your control if she makes a "mistake." Instead, listen and talk with her first. For example, maybe your daughter broke her curfew because the person who agreed to give her a ride home didn't want to leave the party. Instead of immediately grounding her, listen to her explanation and problem solve with her about how she could have handled the situation differently. And remember, sometimes she may not have any choice. She might really be stuck because she couldn't take control at the time. This kind of discussion supports your daughter in the process of making good choices and learning from her mistakes.

* * *

How can you walk the tightrope between too much and too little control? Well, the answer is that you probably can't in a way that will always make your teenage daughter happy. But asking yourself that question from time to time will help you stay on the right track! Even when you know it's time to do some "letting go," you might feel anxious. Parents often mistakenly try to establish greater control when they're feeling threatened or scared, which can leave a teen feeling unfairly limited or treated like a baby. Often, this sets off a power struggle in which nobody wins. It is a mistake to try to take greater control when you are faced with situations in which you should be letting go and exerting less and less control.

As a parent, your real influence does not come from control but from developing a trusting relationship with your daughter. This is a two-way process. You need to earn your daughter's trust, and your daughter needs to know that you are safe to confide in. She needs to feel that you acknowledge her as a separate human being, with her own valuable thoughts and ideas. It will help if your daughter knows that your goal is not to control her life but to work toward developing a mutually trusting relationship.

It helps to acknowledge when you truly don't have control. You might say something like, "I'm not going to be there when you're offered drugs, but I trust that you'll make the right decision for yourself." This goes a long way to help empower your daughter and to help her see that ultimately she needs to be responsible for herself and that you trust her judgment. However, your daughter still needs you as a parent who will exercise appropriate control and limit setting when it's needed. Don't feel pressured into saying yes if you really believe that it's not in your daughter's best interest. Although it might make her angry, your daughter will feel loved and cared about if you provide appropriate limits and exercise control when necessary.

How does competition in adolescent girls compare with competition in adolescent boys? *William L.*

Competition, and learning how to compete, is as important for teenage girls as it is for boys. However, even in today's more egalitarian environment, girls and boys seem to compete in different ways for different reasons and maybe even for different things. Boys are sometimes more comfortable being overtly competitive, as this is often encouraged at an early age in males. Boys are typically less concerned about consensus and are more direct and competitive in their approach. In contrast, girls are often encouraged to be considerate and concerned about other people's feelings and may be less comfortable or even guilty about direct competition. Instead of being direct in their competitive endeavors, girls tend to use consensus building as a way to reach their goals. When competition isn't acknowledged, it can take the form of envy, jealousy, or back-stabbing. Such "passive" competition can inadvertently be more hurtful than direct competition, which often isn't taken so personally. Girls are more likely to be hurt and to be hurtful when they compete indirectly, and when this happens, the issues tend to go on and on rather than getting resolved.

Teens of both sexes can benefit from discussions about competition, which can help them to see that it is normal, important, and healthy to compete. They can learn about the different styles of competition and see that they have choices and options about how to handle their competitive urges in appropriate and responsible ways. The differences in competitive style can create a healthy atmosphere in which girls and boys learn from each other, take the best of the other gender's strategy, and incorporate it into their own. For example, in sports, girls are learning that it is OK and even positive to compete directly and do their best rather than hide their desire to win.

* * *

Even if you are not a sports fanatic, just listening to the news will tell you that women's sports are quickly on the rise. Have you ever seen a women's basketball game on TV? Have you ever watched the Olympics and seen the women's volleyball team? They play hard, they play to win, and they play no differently from the men. No longer are women relegated to the sidelines, where they jump up and down, cheering for the men, waving their pom-poms in the air. Today, women compete, on the field and off. While your daughter may or may not be involved in sports herself, as an adult she will be entering a highly competitive world. Becoming comfortable with competition is important for her future success.

There are definitely stereotypes about how girls compete as compared with boys. Boys are supposed to compete, they are supposed to play to win, and they are taught and reinforced to feel both comfortable and proud when they do win. A certain amount of aggression and entitlement is considered appropriate and manly. When it comes to girls, however, there seem to be two prevailing but very different images. The first one is that girls are passive, meek, weak, and uncomfortable competing at all. These are the girls who feel embarrassed, they don't want to be the center of attention, and they tend to let others win. The second stereotype is that girls who do engage in real competition are catty, bitchy, and back-stabbing. These are the girls who are assumed to be insensitive, uncaring, and clearly not humble enough—or feminine enough. While these two images may be extremes, they highlight the fact that girls are only now learning how to combine their sensitivity and femininity with strength, competitiveness, and drive for success.

Although differences between how girls and boys compete have not entirely disappeared, girls are on the right track. Supporting your daughter in this arena of competition is an important part of building her sense of competence and confidence.

What are reasonable and helpful guidelines that encourage responsibility, especially for housework, school, and finances? *Erica F.*

Now, who in their right mind would *want* to take over unpleasant chores and responsibilities if they didn't have to? Do you look forward to paying the bills? To taking out the garbage? To cleaning the toilets? No way—and if someone offered to do all these chores for you, at no cost, would you resist? Probably not. So, if your daughter is smart, she is going to try to avoid taking on as many unpleasant jobs and responsibilities as she can, for as long as she can. And if she can get you to continue to do them —at no cost to her, why not?

But this is the time when you are *supposed* to be making sure your daughter learns to take on responsibilities for her own life. There are two major factors that operate here. First, as you increase your daughter's responsibilities, you need to give her increased freedom. This makes the whole process more appealing to her. Freedom is the reward for taking on more work. Second, your daughter will be less resistant to taking on more responsibility if you give her responsibilities that she can handle, that she can succeed at, and that make her feel proud. Again, this makes the process more appealing because taking on more and more responsibility is a way to gain more self-esteem and self-respect. So, while your daughter may not want to take on a particular responsibility, the rewards of increased freedom, confidence, and self-respect make it worth doing.

Teens are often very resistant to all the things you try to "make" them do, so it helps both of you if you agree that increased responsibilities go hand in hand with increased freedom. It also helps to explain that your ultimate goal is not to make her miserable doing unpleasant chores but rather to make her feel proud of her increasing ability to be independent and self-sufficient. Finding the right balance, or coming up with guidelines that are reasonable, can best be done in cooperation with your daughter.

If your daughter feels included and is an active participant in these decisions, she is more likely to be motivated to take on and meet her increased responsibilities and less likely to resist or feel controlled. It's a good idea to periodically sit down with your teen and review the balance of responsibilities and freedoms. Talk about how it's going, agree on any changes either one of you may need, and plan ahead for what the next cycle of responsibilities and freedoms will be. Don't forget to give praise for responsibilities done well!

* * *

Some adolescents have a tendency to be overly dependent on their parents. They rely on their parents to check that their homework is done, to nag them about chores, to monitor their school attendance, and to help with their finances. By the time your daughter graduates from high school and moves on to college or work, she needs to be ready to take responsibility for her own schedule, chores, and finances. To make this transition, it is important that during her high school years, you gradually relinquish control while teaching her how to take on more responsibility.

This process of teaching independence and responsibility should begin very early on with such things as small household chores. A young child can set the table or feed the dog. As your daughter gets older, it can help to assign household chores that will have some impact directly on her if they are not done. For example, appropriate chores for your daughter might be preparing her own dinner when you work late, doing her own laundry, or taking care of her room. These chores will have more impact on your daughter than on you, as long as you don't fall into the trap of nagging or rescuing her by doing her chores for her! You may have to get comfortable closing the door to your daughter's room and not thinking about the mess behind the door. Sometimes it is very hard not to respond to pathetic pleas like "I have no clean clothes to wear" when your daughter has not done her laundry as she was supposed to. However, if you consistently respond in a calm, rational way and remind your daughter of her responsibilities without nagging or blaming, she will gradually accept responsibility for completing these tasks.

The same holds true for schoolwork. Your daughter must gradually accept the responsibility for her schoolwork, and you must move from a supervisory role to an advisor who can talk with your daughter about how she is doing in meeting *her* goals in school.

Similarly, the way your daughter will learn to manage her money is by being given increased responsibility and the opportunity to make mistakes with her finances now, when the risks are much smaller than they will be later on. It is a good idea to slowly increase your daughter's allowance or to encourage her to get a part-time job as she gets older. Instead of buying everything for her, give her some financial responsibility. Make it clear that there are additional things she is responsible for buying with the extra money. Many parents expect the additional money to be used for clothing, makeup, or entertainment. It can be very difficult to resist the temptation to bail your daughter out when she is desperate for funds because her budget was unwisely spent. But don't do it! Far too many teens cannot manage their money as young adults because they were not required to do it during their adolescent years.

How do I encourage my daughter to be self-motivated? *Julia Marie T.*

You don't have to encourage your daughter to be self-motivated: She already is! She is already more than happy and motivated to do exactly what *she* wants to do. What you really mean by this question is how do you motivate your daughter to do the things *you* want her to do. In other words, why isn't she motivated to do her homework because you know it's good for her? Why isn't she motivated to pick up the clothes strewn around her bedroom because you want a clean house? Why isn't she volunteering to take on more responsibility because you think she needs to be more responsible?

Look instead at *her* motivations: If she loves tennis, she probably doesn't need much pushing to play tennis. If she loves English, she probably doesn't need much pushing to do her English assignments. If she loves shopping, she probably doesn't need much encouragement to go to the mall. So what you are really asking is how you can help your daughter to want things for herself that she has not yet realized are important to her.

The bottom line is that you can't force this to happen. Be patient. It takes time. And meanwhile, until she has become "self-motivated" in the ways you want her to be, give her support and reward her for doing the things that you want her to do, like homework or chores.

* * *

Self-motivation is a gradual process and won't happen all at once. Different kids develop the skills necessary for self-motivation at different times in their lives, so it is important not to get too frustrated if your daughter seems delayed in this area. When adolescents feel that others are in charge of their lives and are there to take care of everything so nothing too bad will happen to them, they have a tendency to take on less responsibility. If you place a reasonable amount of responsibility on your daughter, she is likely to spend more time carefully considering the decisions she makes. She will become more self-motivated and less dependent on others. However, while many parents *know* all of this, it is much easier said than done.

It's hard to allow your daughter to make mistakes. You naturally want to try to protect her from all the mistakes you can. So, think about the responsibilities you have given your daughter. And think about whether you really should still be reminding her about homework, checking to be sure her laundry has been done, that her lunch has been packed, that she has her supplies ready for the next day. During the teen years, you must continue to assume responsibility for seeing that your daughter takes care of some things. However, for many things, the consequences are not so severe that your daughter can't be allowed to make mistakes. If she didn't do the laundry, which was her job, and she has to wear crumpled clothing to school for a day or two, she is more likely to get the laundry done the next time. She will learn the importance of planning ahead so she has clean clothes. If you rescue her, by reminding her of the laundry until it gets done, doing it yourself, or letting her borrow your clean clothes, she will only learn to continue to depend on you to prevent problems and certainly won't become self-motivated to do the laundry. As your daughter directly experiences the consequences of her behavior, she is more likely to become self-motivated to take care of her responsibilities.

Hot Tips

☞ If you want your daughter to talk to you, start by looking at how well you listen to her. Listening means not interrupting her; listening means not criticizing her. It means that your body language does not judge or discount what she is saying. Listening is not an easy skill to learn. It takes practice.

☞ Good communication comes in the context of an ongoing relationship. Time spent together, where spontaneous conversation can happen, provides the foundation for good communication. You cannot rely only on scheduled time to talk with your daughter. The best talks are often unplanned.

☞ Don't use guilt as a way to try to get your daughter to talk to you. Questions like "Why don't you ever talk to me?" won't work.

☞ Most teenage rebellion is healthy. Your daughter's *normal* need to rebel does not have to result in constant friction between you. Healthy rebellion is a necessary and important part of your daughter's passage into adulthood. It means that she is becoming her own person!

☞ Age-appropriate limits, which you decide on with your daughter, along with reasonable consequences for breaking those limits, are some of the best ways to support your daughter's normal need to challenge your authority.

☞ There is a difference between discipline and punishment. The goal of disciplining your daughter is to teach her that there are consequences for her behavior. The goal of punishment is to hurt, to cause pain. Punishment almost always leads to the desire for revenge and rarely teaches the person anything. So, when you are deciding how to deal with misbehavior or broken rules, don't make it your goal to cause her pain, even if you are furious. Instead, discipline her by imposing a consequence that will *teach* her something, and make this a learning experience.

☞ The reality is that adolescent girls are more vulnerable to physical danger than boys are. Therefore, it is sometimes appropriate to be more "restrictive" about where your daughter can go and how late she can be out. But be careful that your restrictions are not simply gender stereotypes, that you have good reasons for giving your daughter different rules than her brother or than you would an adolescent boy. Admit that you are treating her differently, and explain your reasons to her.

☞ Your daughter's mood swings are probably normal! And, while you don't have to like or accept *how* she might be expressing her feelings, let her know that you are available to listen and you can accept *what* she feels. While your daughter shouldn't be allowed to take out her feelings on other people, she is entitled to have her feelings, and you should not judge them. But if your daughter seems to be having severe and constant mood swings, talk to a professional.

☞ While it may be hard to accept, your daughter is *supposed* to distance herself from her family as she gets older. As this happens, you might feel like she has no time or interest in her family at all. However, no matter how it may seem at the moment, your family is as important to your daughter now as it has always been. Instead of insisting or demanding that your daughter spend the same amount and kinds of family time as she used to, work with her to set up some designated "family times." Although these times might not be as often as you might like, they will help you and your daughter feel like she is still connected with the family.

☞ Most shouting matches between you and your daughter are probably about rules, grades, household responsibilities, or money. One of the ways you can reduce the number of these types of arguments is for you to not be so "trigger happy" with your own anger. Most of the time, your anger comes from feelings of concern or worry about your daughter. Try talking directly with your daughter about these feelings. And encourage your daughter to talk about *her* feelings. Then, your daughter is more likely to seriously listen to what you have to say.

☞ Anger is a normal feeling! And it's not *feeling* angry that is the problem; it's *how* we do or don't express our anger. It is important and healthy for you and your daughter to be able to express anger. Anger that is not expressed builds up and often comes out in the form of an explosion. Anger that is not expressed can lead to depression. Your daughter needs ways to express her anger. Think about how you are a role model for the expression of anger in your family. What are the ways your daughter is allowed to express her anger? Can she raise her voice, slam her door, or call a friend to let off some steam? Everyone needs ways to express their anger!

☞ While it may be difficult having your daughter constantly challenge you, it is necessary and important. It means that she is learning how to trust and believe in herself and her own judgments. And, while you may have wisdom that only comes with experience, your daughter is growing up in a different world. This means that you need to listen to her challenges and think about them carefully before you reject them.

☞ Failure is a part of growing up. Your daughter

might express huge feelings of upset when she encounters failure. Listen! Let her vent! Don't trivialize her feelings! And don't lecture her about how she might have avoided failing. Be supportive, and let her know you care about how bad she feels.

☞ When it comes to sexual knowledge, your daughter can't have too much! While it may be difficult for you to talk with your daughter about sex, in today's world it is a must! Provide your daughter with ongoing and accurate information. Give her the resources to answer her questions. Talk to her about her concerns. *It could save her life!*

☞ It is your "job" to set limits and your daughter's "job" to try to break them. The idea is to slowly replace your control with negotiation and compromise. Allow for mistakes, and use them as learning experiences. While your daughter's physical safety is something you should never compromise, there are many other areas where you *can* negotiate and compromise.

☞ Competition and learning how to compete are as important for adolescent girls as they are for boys. Don't discourage your daughter from healthy competition. Don't make her feel that being a girl means she should not be competitive. Healthy competition helps us to do our best.

☞ Responsibility does not develop overnight. It is learned over time. Start early, and slowly increase your expectations. Work together with your daughter to decide what responsibilities she will have. Be open to changing things as her life changes. Remember that your daughter's first job is her schoolwork. But don't forget that she needs time for her friends and time for herself as well.

☞ When your daughter was younger, her motivation to do things like her homework and chores came mostly from her desire to please you. As your daughter moves into adulthood, allow her to begin to experience the natural consequences of her actions so that her motivation shifts from pleasing you to pleasing herself. This shift is an essential part of growing up. Let her gradually learn from the consequences of her own actions.

2

Why Can't She Ever Think for Herself?
Adolescent Girls and Their Peer Group

When our daughter Kara was younger, she had a mind of her own. Her teachers always described her as being self-assured and an independent thinker. We were always so very proud of her for that. But now that she's a teenager, it seems like most of the time she's either worried about or consumed with what her friends are thinking or doing. She can't seem to make a simple decision without talking to at least three or four friends. All she seems to think about is what her friends will think and what they're doing, and, of course, *boys*. Boys, boys, boys! It seems like boys have suddenly become the center of our daughter's life! We're really afraid that she's losing any sense of her own identity and is just following the crowd.

As parents, we find ourselves worrying about Kara a lot these days—especially those times when her friends seem to be treating her so poorly. She used to be proud of who she was, of being unique. But now she almost always tries to melt into this "group image." Our daughter's a smart kid, but sometimes it seems as if she's acting dumb on purpose. She used be involved in sports—she loved softball. She would never even miss a practice. Now it seems like she'd just rather hang out with her girlfriends. We just don't understand how anyone can spend so much time at the mall.

We don't want Kara to always be a follower, but it seems like we're powerless to get her to see what she's doing. And we can't understand why she hides who she really is. We know she can think for herself. She's got to learn how to make good choices and decisions, but she won't even buy a pair of jeans without discussing it with 10 of her best friends.

How can we trust that Kara will ever learn how to make good decisions for herself when she can't seem to be her own person? We're worried about what she's getting involved in and how her friends' influence might just send her in the wrong direction. We don't want to control our daughter, we just want to protect her, but we don't seem to have much influence anymore.

—*Frank and Bernice, parents of Kara, age 14*

How can I convince my daughter not to follow the "in crowd"? *Hannah A.*

It is important to realize that it is completely natural for your daughter to want to follow the "in crowd." During the teen years, "belonging" and "fitting in" become very important. As your daughter slowly moves away from her family being the focus of her life, it is normal for her to look for a "family of peers" to make her feel that she belongs. At the same time (although she may not realize it), it is important for your daughter to hold on to her own identity and not make her entire life revolve around fitting in.

If you feel your daughter is severely limiting herself by trying to follow the in crowd, try to encourage her to broaden her friendships. If there is a church or temple youth group, suggest she give it a try. Getting your daughter involved with group activities that reflect her interests and talents is another way to help her expand her friendships and expose her to greater diversity. Doing volunteer work is a very rewarding way for teens to meet kids outside of their immediate friendship group.

Encouraging your daughter's hobbies and interests, where she will experience her competence and gain confidence, will go a long way toward providing her with the strength she needs to resist following the whims of others. Teens who build their self-esteem by getting involved in activities that reflect their unique skills and talents are more likely to be able to resist following the in crowd all the time.

Don't criticize or attack the in group. Instead, encourage and support your daughter to expand on rather than eliminate her friendships.

* * *

Don't get fooled into thinking that just because your daughter is becoming more independent that she doesn't still need time with her family. One of the ways many parents inadvertently encourage their daughters to follow the crowd is by not pursuing their *own* relationships with their daughters. Recent research has shown that the more time adolescents spend with their families, the less likely they are to engage in self-destructive behaviors. So, while your daughter may be resistant, and you need to be careful not to demand too much time with her, it is crucial that you insist on spending some quality time together.

Don't approach this time together as a chance to hold an inquisition! This is about fun, sharing, and enjoying each other's company. And, of course, if a serious discussion emerges, that would be fine too! With today's hectic pace, it might be difficult to arrange a lot of family time during which everyone joins in. But mother–daughter or father–daughter activities, just as a twosome, are extremely valuable. Another way of arranging time together is by joining together with other families or joining in other mother–daughter or father–daughter group activities.

Don't forget that your daughter will learn from what you do much more than from what you say. In fact, she may examine your behavior with a fine-toothed comb. If it hasn't happened to you yet, watch out for the time when you suggest something to your daughter and she confronts you with the fact that often you don't follow your own advice. So, look at your own behavior: Do you model a willingness to be different? Do you have more than one group of friends? Are all your friends alike? Are you overly influenced by your peer groups? Do you get involved in activities that are "different"?

In the end, you cannot control or choose your daughter's friends. But you can encourage, model, and teach by example. Whatever you do, unless you have a very good, concrete reason, don't "forbid" your daughter to be friends with someone. This will only backfire by making her angry at you and protective of her friends.

How can I help my daughter not make boys the focus of her existence and not see herself through guys' eyes? *Mikayla C.*

During the teen years, a certain amount of focus on boys is normal and natural. Just like the "terrible twos," this is a stage that your daughter will likely outgrow. If your daughter does not have a variety of sources of self-esteem, she is more likely to become overly focused on boys. This is particularly true for teens who struggle with school or don't feel they have the opportunity to shine through their other talents or skills. Helping your daughter to succeed academically and supporting her involvement in activities in which she can be successful can go a long way toward helping her to not depend solely on guys for validation.

If you see your daughter being too concerned about what boys think of her, direct criticism of her seldom works. She is much more likely to respond to gentle questions about her behavior. For example, if you think your daughter is wearing a dress that is too seductive, you might ask her, "Why did you pick that dress? Do you feel good about yourself when you wear it? Is it something that you are wearing for yourself, or because of the reaction other people will have?" Sometimes the responses to the questions you ask won't be the answers you wanted to hear. However, after you have listened to her reasons, and possibly carefully voiced your own opinion, respect your daughter's right to make her own choices. Even if your daughter doesn't change her behavior, she is more likely to think about what you said if you didn't make it into a confrontation or criticism. It is your respect of your daughter's decision making as she grows up that builds her self-esteem and gives her the strength to see herself through her own eyes rather than to depend on boys' opinions.

* * *

While most girls eventually outgrow being totally focused on guys and develop a better balance between their interest in guys and other parts of their lives, some girls don't outgrow this stage very easily, and in fact might get stuck in it. Girls who grow up with "absentee fathers," or fathers who do not take the time to acknowledge them, or fathers who do not provide them with positive feedback for their skills, talents, and femininity, are often desperately in need of male attention. So, it is important for teenage girls to have adult males who validate them and make them feel good about themselves. If your daughter does not have a father who is actively involved in her life, help her connect with uncles, grandfathers, older cousins, teachers, coaches, or other men who can serve as sources of self-esteem for her.

* * *

How many teen or women's magazines have you seen lately? Although there are some magazines that focus on women's careers and accomplishments, far too many continue to emphasize how girls or women can attract men! This is particularly true of magazines marketed to teenage girls. The covers feature gorgeous models wearing sexy, skimpy clothes and give instructions on how to kiss, seduce, attract, and keep a man! Look at the feature articles: How to get the man of your dreams... How to know if boys think you're sexy... How to find Mr. Right... and so on. So, since many aspects of our culture give your daughter the message that she should see herself through a guy's eyes and focus her existence on boys, you have a big job ahead of you. You have to try and undo a major influence in her life.

But the good news is you are not totally helpless. In spite of the media, you can have a significant impact on your daughter's way of seeing herself. First, point out to her how the media is influencing her. And ask her if she really wants to be spending so much of her time and energy trying to please and attract guys. Many teen girls don't even realize how they are buying into or being led by the media. Once they realize it, they are much more open to preventing this from happening. Second, if you are a mother, take a look at the magazines *you* buy, and how much time and energy *you* put into focusing on men. Whether you realize it or not, adolescent girls who view their mothers as dependent on male attention for their self-esteem will often follow the same path. If you are a father, remember that teen girls whose fathers give them the message that women are supposed to attract and please men are communicating to their daughters that they should build their self-esteem on how guys see them.

So, examine your own behavior and values. Take a look at what you might inadvertently be communicating to your daughter. Make sure that you don't buy into the media stereotypes.

How can I help my adolescent daughter believe in herself more and not worry so much about what her peers think?
Vanessa S.

Your daughter's ability to believe in herself and think for herself is directly connected to her self-esteem. Because self-esteem has its origins in the views others have of us, it is natural for your daughter to look to her peer group for affirmation. When her peer group thinks highly of her, she is more likely to think highly of herself. Therefore, it is quite normal for your daughter's friends to become increasingly important to her during her teen years. The multiple opinions of her friends, along with her parents, teachers, and other adults, all help your daughter to define herself and develop her own unique identity.

Don't jump to conclude that all of your daughter's behaviors and choices are motivated by what her peers think. Just because you don't agree with her doesn't mean she has *only* been influenced by her peers. She may just be making choices that you disagree with! And, while you may not like or approve of some of the values, clothing choices, or behaviors of her friends, it is important not to verbalize strong negative opinions about them.

The best way to help your daughter believe more

in herself is by encouraging her to consider her own values, needs, and feelings in making choices about things such as activities, makeup, and clothes. Stay away from absolute comments about "right" and "wrong," "bad" and "good," or "stupid" and "smart" whenever possible. For example, suppose your daughter has been involved in an activity like ice-skating for many years. Suddenly she announces to you that she wants to give it up because she doesn't have time and none of her friends are interested in skating. Ask her to think about whether she will miss skating and to think about a way she might still fit it into her schedule. Tell your daughter about something you do that none of your friends do, and how glad you are that you haven't given up this activity. Suggest that she think about her decision for a few days, and then get back to you. Although in the end you can't force her, giving your daughter some things to consider might help her to think more for herself and not be so controlled by what her peers think and do.

Remember that it is really hard for your daughter to balance her need to be accepted by her peers with her need to be her unique self. By fostering open conversations, giving your daughter things to think about, or even suggesting how she might balance her life, you are providing her with the skills to make good decisions and to believe in herself.

* * *

Most people, not just teenagers, are concerned about what their peers think. We all want to fit in and belong. The issue is one of balance: How much do we allow the desire to "fit in" control how we think and behave?

You can help your daughter to find the right balance. To begin with, watch your tone of voice and how you communicate with her. If you are not judgmental and express compassion and understanding about how hard it can be to stand apart from "the group," your daughter is more likely to listen to what you say. Then she can begin to make honest comparisons of her needs, values, and beliefs with those of her peer group. If you can, share with her a time when you remember being very caught up with peers, either as an adolescent or as an adult. Tell her how you did or didn't follow the group and what you learned from the experience. As she makes these comparisons for herself, your daughter will begin to worry less and less about the opinions of her friends. Her worry will be replaced by confidence in her own convictions and an increased ability to make difficult choices.

The key here is to be compassionate and understanding, not critical. Comments like "Why don't you think for yourself?" or "If all your friends decided to jump off a bridge, would you follow them?" certainly won't help. They will just make your daughter angry and defensive. Instead, try comments that begin with words like, "I understand..." or "It must be hard..." or "I know you're worried about what your friends are going to think." Recognizing your daughter's feelings and not giving her the message that you think she is weak or just a follower will go a long way toward helping her examine her own views and balance them with what her peers think.

How can I help foster independence and self-worth and not have my daughter depend on someone else (like a boyfriend) for her identity? *Emma V.*

Helping your daughter to become more independent and to value herself is the most important gift you can give her. However, lecturing her about the importance of being independent won't help. It will only make her feel criticized and misunderstood. The best way to support your daughter's growing independence is through daily experiences that teach her responsibility and help her to learn decision-making skills. Whenever possible, allow and encourage your daughter to make her own choices regarding schoolwork, bedtime, personal attire, dating, and so on. The goal is not to make sure your daughter doesn't make any mistakes but to patiently support her through her successes and mistakes. As your daughter develops her confidence in handling increased responsibilities and in decision making, her ability to think and act independently will increase and her self-worth will improve. However, remember that issues of popularity, status, and the desire to please her friends or boyfriend are normal and will continually challenge your daughter.

To have a relationship that will foster your daughter's independence and self-worth, don't punish her for making honest mistakes. Your goal is for her to learn from her mistakes, not to fear making mistakes so much that she cannot take the steps she needs to become more independent. However, blatant disregard for the rules, or deliberately ignoring her responsibilities, is another matter. Then, some form of discipline may be needed. But in either case, the goal is to help your daughter figure out what she really feels and what she really wants for herself. It is only through this process that she can eventually become independent.

If you see your daughter as overly dependent on someone (like a boyfriend) for her identity, don't try to break up or limit the relationship by force or arbitrary rules. That strategy is likely to backfire. Instead, encourage your daughter to spend time with her other friends and point out to her how important it is not to ignore them. For example, you can remind her that if things don't go well with her boyfriend, she'll probably need her other friends a lot.

Independence comes through increased responsibility. If your daughter does not have the chance to make her own decisions, she will always look to others to make them for her.

* * *

Close your eyes and take a minute to think back to when your daughter was taking her first steps. Remember how excited you were? But of course, it took a while until she went from those first steps to being able to truly walk independently. No matter how hard you might have tried to teach her or encourage her, she walked when she was ready. Not a day sooner.

Well, developing self-worth and independence is a similar process. It takes time and practice. As much as you might want to rush the process, becoming responsible and independent does not happen overnight. It is a slow process. With each new challenge, and with each new situation, there are new skills your daughter has to learn.

Keep reminding yourself that your daughter's identity is still emerging. Be patient. Remember that just as the rate of physical growth varies, so does the rate of emotional growth: Some girls simply take longer than others to develop their independence and self-worth.

Particularly during the middle school years, some girls remain very unsure of themselves, whereas others seem to be blossoming and demonstrating increased independence and self-confidence. But, even allowing for the slower pace of some girls, by the time your daughter is about 16 years old, or a junior in high school, you should begin to see her developing greater independence from the behaviors and opinions of her friends. If you don't see these changes and she seems "stuck," or if you see her as having very low self-worth, it's time to take action. Some signs of low self-worth include constantly making negative comments about her skills, her opinions, or her appearance; resistance to trying any new activity or experience; and defensiveness and irritability when asked to leave her "comfort zone." If you notice these signs, you should seek professional help. Don't wait until things get worse.

Do friends have a great deal of influence on my adolescent daughter? *Jerry J.*

You bet they do! Friends have a lot of influence on your daughter, and often for the better. Your daughter's social development requires that she learn to choose friends who are fun to be with and who make her feel good about herself. The abilities to form trusting relationships, to love someone who is not exactly the same as you, and to feel that you belong all originate from friendships. In addition, it is through friendships that teens learn to handle social conflicts and resolve interpersonal problems. So, there are many important and valuable ways that your daughter is positively influenced by her friends. However, there are also many struggles and temptations that emanate from teen friendships. This is where you, as a parent, can play a critical role. You can be an emotional anchor when your daughter's friendships cause her great distress or hardship.

If you want to be seen as a resource for your daughter, you have to lay the groundwork that makes it possible for her to be open to your help and support when she needs it. If you choose your battles wisely and give her plenty of choice and freedom on issues that are a matter of taste, rather than safety, your daughter will more likely see you as a valuable resource. In addition, your daughter will be more likely to seek you out and consider your opinion and perspective about other issues and choices in her life. So, while your daughter's friends definitely have a great deal of influence on her, this does not mean that you automatically become irrelevant. Your ability to influence your daughter depends on the relationship you have developed with her. Resist the temptation to be overly controlling and overprotective. Listen before you speak, and in general, if you are not sure that your advice or opinion is wanted, ask. Accept honest mistakes as part of her development and use discipline when it is called for, not simply to take revenge when you are angry. Remember to enjoy your daughter's teen years—they will be gone before you know it.

* * *

Not only are friends an important part of being a teenager, but they are also critical for healthy development. It is more worrisome when a teenager has no real friends and is isolated and alone than if she has a tough time managing the influences of friends. Teens who are withdrawn and have few social relationships with peers cannot develop a feeling of competence and self-worth in relationships. No one develops his or her self-worth in a vacuum. Interactions with others, learning from others, and resisting the influences of others are part of the normal maturation process.

If your daughter does not seem to naturally develop at least some friendships, your direct intervention may be needed. Telling your daughter to try talking to more people or sitting at a lunch table where there are other kids won't work. If she had the self-esteem or confidence to do these things, she would have already done them! Instead, look for specific activities or groups she can join, like a church youth group, a hiking club, or a volunteer effort that includes other teens. Look beyond her school or immediate neighborhood where she may already have a reputation for being a loner. Helping your daughter to locate a group of kids who share her interests is a good way to support her in developing friendships. It is OK to be fairly insistent that she at least *try* one of these groups or activities. But after she has given it a fair try, it is really her decision about whether to continue or not. With help and guidance, just about all teens can find someplace where they fit in and can find friends. It is only through experiences with friends that your daughter will be able to develop her social skills.

Is it OK that my 16-year-old daughter no longer wants to spend time at home with the family? She wants to be with her boyfriend. When she is home, she spends her time in her room. *Allison H.*

It sounds like your daughter is branching out into a life of her own with people of her choice outside her immediate family. By spending time in her room, your daughter is learning to be alone and enjoy her own company and her privacy. These behaviors are normal and OK unless your daughter *never* wants to be with the family. The privacy helps your daughter get away from the constant public scrutiny many teens feel during the day. Often, home becomes the only place that "being on" does not feel like a requirement. By spending time in her room, your daughter may simply be emotionally and socially "resting"; don't take it as a personal rejection. Instead, try stopping by her room once in a while, just to say hello. But, if your daughter is hiding from painful problems, that's another story, and she will need your help and guidance.

If you want your daughter to spend more time with the family, offer opportunities—but don't force the issue. Be insistent only when family activities are very significant or important to you, such as a particular holiday, the wedding of a good friend, the funeral of a close or elderly relative, an infrequently held family reunion, or a special church event. Perhaps family time needs to be structured. Inviting your daughter to an activity that has a clear beginning and end, so that she does not fear getting stuck, may reduce some of her resistance to spending time with the family.

If you believe that your daughter's boyfriend is taking all of her time away from the family, remember that the excitement of a boyfriend and the wish to be with him as much as possible is not in itself an indication that something is wrong. If you want your daughter to spend more time with the family, then try inviting her boyfriend to join you for meals, a family activity, or just to "hang out" at your house. Communicating to your daughter that you are not always asking her to choose between her family and her boyfriend will not only give you more time with her but will also give you a chance to meet and get to know her boyfriend better. If the time spent with family is fun and enjoyable, your daughter will increasingly choose to devote at least some of her time to be with you.

* * *

If your daughter is not only spending all her time in her room or with her boyfriend but also seems to respond with irritation, annoyance, or negativity whenever you approach her, she may be hiding from painful problems, and she will need your help and guidance. It is possible that she is running away from problems in her personal life. Is she failing in school? Are her friends ridiculing her? Is her boyfriend the only person she feels she can trust? Or, your daughter may be trying to escape from family tensions that are unpleasant to her. Take a look at how the members of your family relate to each other and to your daughter. Is there constant arguing? Or teasing? Is everyone always bickering? Does a brother or sister demand and get most of the attention? Or are there even more serious family problems, like alcoholism or abuse?

Whether she is trying to avoid personal problems or problems in the family, your daughter will not readily choose to be at home with the family unless things change. And don't think you can hide or sugarcoat the problems: Most teens are very perceptive. So whether the problem rests solely with your daughter or involves one or more members of the family, you have to address the problems directly.

To begin with, try talking to your daughter about why she doesn't want to spend time at home with the family. Begin by asking her if there is anything that you or other family members are doing to make her feel unwanted, unappreciated, or upset. By first asking your daughter how others might be hurting her, you are letting her know that you are concerned about her feelings, rather than simply trying to get her to do something that you want and she doesn't!

If the issues are about the family, try calling a family meeting and discussing the problems. Make a rule that each person gets up to 5 minutes to talk without being interrupted before a back-and-forth discussion begins. Give your daughter lots of support for being willing to talk about what is bothering her.

Don't dispute her point of view and don't tell her she is wrong. Instead, look for ways that you and other members of the family can help her feel more comfortable.

If your daughter's issues have more to do with her personal life, try to talk with her in ways that make her feel safe enough to tell you what is going on. Let her know that you are available to help her in any way, and that as a parent who loves and cares about her, you cannot simply let her isolation from the family continue for a long time. It's OK to give your daughter some time and space to solve her problems, either with or without your help, but don't allow her to totally disconnect from the family.

Finally, if the problems continue, whether they are with the family or with your daughter's personal problems, *get help*. Family counselors or individual therapists who specialize in working with adolescents can be located through your local mental health association, church or synagogue, or local hospital.

How can we help adolescent girls be friends with boys without feeling the pressure to do the emotional caretaking?
Amanda E.

Boys and girls alike learn how to behave with each other by imitating the adults around them. If girls see their mothers as doing all the "emotional caretaking" (meaning that they put their own emotions on the back burner and focus on ensuring that everyone else is happy), then they will more likely come to believe that this is what women are supposed to do. In the same vein, if boys grow up seeing their fathers expecting their wives to take care of them, they will expect girls to take care of them as well. Parents, teachers, and other adults serve as the role models that tell our daughters how they are supposed to treat boys and men.

If you believe that your daughter feels like she is "supposed" to be the emotional caretaker for guys, think about what might be motivating her to behave this way. Is it possible that this is the only way she believes that a boy will like her? Or, is it her indirect way of asking for attention? Most likely, there is someone in her home environment, usually (but not always) her mother, who has taken on the role of caretaker and is forever taking care of the "helpless" other family members. Ask yourself if you are, by your behavior, teaching your daughter that either men are helpless in the home or that they are simply supposed to be taken care of? Does your daughter get the message that the only way to get a man's approval is to take care of his every need?

Ask your daughter to think about whether or not she is feeling taken care of by the guy friends or boyfriend whom she spends time with. Help her examine how equal things are. Talk with her about what she thinks guys expect from her, and ask her what she expects from guys. Explore with your daughter how she perceives the role models in your own home. Even though it may be difficult to hear, don't deny her feedback if it is really true. The most powerful way you can have an impact on your daughter's ideas about relationships is through your own behavior. Impress on your daughter that healthy relationships, particularly those with men, are built on give and take, not on one person doing all the giving and the other doing all the taking.

* * *

When a girl is simply "friends" with a guy, she is less likely to feel pressured to do the emotional caretaking than when she wants the friendship to develop into a romance. Many girls are able to be "equals" in a friendship, but when they are involved in a love relationship, they lose the balance and become caretakers—sometimes they even go so far as to take care of all his friends as well! Unless your daughter feels she has enough to offer, so that she can insist that the relationship be an equal give and take, she will be tempted to buy into the cultural stereotype that women should take care of men.

Take a moment to think about the differences between the amounts of emotional support that men and women provide for each other. Most men have a harder time giving emotional support, or even noticing when it's needed, than women do. This is not necessarily because they don't care as much but rather because, unlike women who were taught to feel good about themselves based on what they do for others, men have been taught to gain their self-esteem through their own achievements and successes. Therefore, many men do not pick up on a woman's need for emotional help or support and don't feel competent in doing the emotional caretaking.

While this explains the differences between men and women, *it is by no means* something that you want your daughter to accept. Adolescent girls whose parents and other adult role models communicate the importance of equality in a relationship are less likely to become emotional caretakers. The best way to help adolescent girls not feel pressured to do the emotional caretaking is to provide them with role models of equality and point out to them when they are doing too much for the other person.

It can be helpful to encourage your daughter to start a relationship with a friendship first, rather than jumping right into a romance. In this way, she can more easily start off with a basis of equality and might be able to maintain a better balance when a romance develops.

Help your daughter, too, to understand that men often have a harder time responding emotionally. Therefore, one of the ways that girls can help pursue equality is to speak up and let the guy know how they feel and what they need. The idea that guys can guess what women want is just not true. While guys need to learn how to be better emotional caretakers, women need to learn how to communicate their needs more clearly and directly.

How can I help my teenage daughter maintain high self-esteem in the face of cruelty from peers? *Elizabeth N.*

If your daughter comes home and tells you that friends or classmates are being cruel to her, start by being compassionate and empathetic, and listen carefully to her story. Determine if the cruelty is so extreme that it warrants your intervention. In most cases, while your daughter's experience is clearly very upsetting to her, it is not seriously dangerous or damaging to her long-term emotional or physical health. In fact, most cruelty among girls consists of name calling, "back stabbing" with words, ignoring someone and leaving them out of the group, and betraying trust. Physical cruelty among girls is much less common.

Help your daughter understand that people who are mean to other people generally don't feel very good about themselves. While it may not be obvious on the outside, most kids who are cruel or bully other kids are actually very insecure themselves. Although these explanations won't change your daughter's experience, they will help give her some perspective, which is the beginning of her healing from her wounds.

It is important to help your daughter understand that as hard as it might be, she cannot passively accept cruelty from peers, or from anyone else. She must hold others accountable for how they treat her. When someone steps "over the line," your daughter needs to understand the importance of not permitting them to take advantage of her. She can stand up for herself by speaking up and being forthright. At first, your daughter might not have the courage to do this on her own. So, help her to determine whom she can call on for assistance. Perhaps one of her friends can "back her up" in confronting the "enemy." As your daughter develops more confidence and actively speaks up when others step over the line, she will be less vulnerable to cruelty from peers.

Another way to help your daughter is to have her consider the possibility that sometimes the most powerful response is one that includes no words, just body language. She can hold her head up, look her peers straight in the eyes, and then walk away. While she might at first view this way of responding as passive and "giving in," help her see that sometimes this can be the most assertive and effective way for her to stand up for herself. By behaving as if the cruelty of peers has no effect on her whatsoever, she interrupts the cycle because she is no longer giving them the response they want.

It can really be heartbreaking to see your daughter suffer, but resist your temptation to jump in and rescue her because it will ultimately bolster her self-esteem much more if your daughter can handle the problem without your intervention.

* * *

While it may be hard to imagine, some teens "invite" cruelty because they have too strong a need to be liked by everyone. Therefore, they are willing to tolerate being mistreated, abused, and even victimized because they are afraid to risk the possibility of *not* being liked. Because they are so desperate to be liked, and other kids see them as weak, they become easy targets for bullying, ridicule, and harassment.

These are the kids who believe that the path to being accepted involves pleasing others, no matter what the cost. They have convinced themselves that being treated poorly is better than being ignored, and they make excuses for the other person's misdeeds. Over time, their willingness to accept mistreatment slowly erodes their self-esteem even further, and they become less and less capable of finding the strength to defend themselves.

In order to break out of this kind of vicious cycle, your daughter needs help in understanding how her desperate need to be liked is directly connected to being treated cruelly. She needs to know that nobody is going to treat her better than she treats herself. For example, in order to gain the respect of others, your daughter has to feel *entitled* to be respected. Until she understands this connection, she will not be able to stand up for herself.

Impress on your daughter that no matter who she is, or how hard she tries, not everyone is going to like her. It is not a negative reflection on her worth as a person if someone doesn't admire her. To take good care of herself, your daughter needs to like and respect herself enough so that she can give up the unreachable goal of having everyone else like her or be her friend.

* * *

Self-esteem or a solid sense of self-value begins very early in life, way before peers enter the picture. If your daughter has low self-esteem (in other words, if she often feels inadequate or that she is a failure, or if she is constantly disappointed in herself and feels she doesn't measure up), she will be especially vulnerable to cruelty from peers. In some instances, this cruelty can be so hurtful and can go on for such a long time that serious emotional damage is done.

While there are a number of reasons that a girl gets "picked on," one of the most frequent is her looks, particularly her weight or breast development. Girls who don't look like their peers can experience years of harassment, tormenting, and ridicule. And parents often feel helpless and hopeless in stemming the tide of cruelty.

While you certainly can't control the other kids, you can support your daughter by giving her ideas about how she can disengage from the cruel peers, choose more deserving friends, and ask for help when she needs it. If your daughter is overweight, offer to take her to a nutritionist or join a weight loss program or gym. If breast development is the problem, see if you can shop with her and help select bras and clothing that minimize her being "different." Be careful not to criticize her or make her feel weak or helpless. And don't dismiss her experience as just "part of growing up." While we all know that most kids experience cruelty from peers at some point during their teen years, be aware that constant cruelty can take its toll on your daughter's emotional health and she might need professional help. You might even need to consider more drastic action, like enrolling her in a different school.

Why do some teenage girls feel they have to act like an "air head" or "dumb down" to get boys to like them? *Sophia Y.*

The idea that females need to act like they are less intelligent than males to get males to like them has been around for a long time. In spite of the women's movement and feminism, some girls continue to "play dumb," believing that this is the only way to attract and keep a guy. These girls are careful not to let their smarts or talents show through. They don't believe that guys want to have anything to do with girls who might be smarter or better than them in any way. They think that guys need to feel one-up to be attracted to and stick with a girl. Many of these girls know they are acting dumb, but they don't care because they think it is going to attract a guy.

Most often, these girls have learned to behave this way from watching other women flirt with men by playing dumb and making the guy feel like a big shot or really cool. If your daughter seems to feel that she has to act like an airhead or "dumb down" to get a boy to like her, it's time for a serious talk. Tell her directly how important it is that she not view men as though they are better or more entitled than herself. Emphasize to her that girls are as good as guys and that hiding who she is won't make her happy in the long run. If your own behavior with men has contributed to your daughter's behavior, admit to her that you wish you had known better when you were younger. Show her the ways in which you are working to change your own behavior. This is the most powerful way you can begin to help your daughter to accept her strengths and behave as an equal with guys.

For some girls, acting like an airhead or dumbing down reflects a much deeper problem. These are the girls who have very low self-esteem and only value themselves in terms of male attention. Often these girls have difficulty setting limits on what guys want from them. They might use drugs or alcohol in self-destructive ways to please a guy. They may also not respect their own boundaries about sexual behavior because they think they've got to do whatever the guy wants. These girls need lots of help to gain the self-esteem necessary to break their dependence on guys. These girls feel desperate and fear that they will lose a guy if they don't lower themselves in order to continually make him feel smarter and better. And for them, the thought of losing the guy is intolerable.

These girls are in big trouble and need professional help in order to find ways to feel better about themselves and boost their self-esteem. They also may need closer parental supervision because they are more likely to engage in high risk, self-destructive behavior.

* * *

Although it might appear to you that some girls act like airheads or dummies, at times you might be misinterpreting what you see. What some adults might see as dumbing down can actually be a girl's attempt to be funny and friendly with guys. A girl might act this way with a guy she really likes because it makes her feel less anxious when she is first trying to get to know him. Often, girls use humor and joking, rather than serious discussion, as a way to ease into a relationship. A girl might joke around and seem to be acting like an airhead in order not to scare the guy away until she has a chance of getting connected with him. (Younger teens might behave this way longer, because they are still developing the confidence and skills to interact with boys.) Once the girl is connected, however, she is able to be herself and act as smart as she really is. She is even able to compete with the guy, and enjoy it, without feeling threatened that he will no longer like her. So, don't jump to conclusions. Give it some time. But if you don't see your daughter showing all her smarts and talents pretty soon, you need to have a serious talk with her.

Why does my adolescent daughter wear "weird stuff"? *Mike O.*

To begin with, you've got to remember that what *you* think is weird is not weird to your daughter. And, if you constantly criticize and judge your daughter's way of dressing, she will feel like you don't respect her right to have her own form of self-expression through her clothes.

During the teen years, girls are trying to decide who they are and where they fit in. They use their clothes, makeup, and jewelry as a means of communicating who they are and how they want other people to relate to them. While some or all of your daughter's outfits might seem distasteful to you, don't get caught up in her style of dressing. What is far more important is how your daughter is functioning in important areas of her life. Is she working at an acceptable level academically? Is her behavior within the family and at school appropriate? Is she meeting her basic responsibilities? Do you feel assured that she is not engaging in high-risk or self-destructive behaviors? If your answer to all of these questions is "yes," lay off commenting about her appearance and save your battles for serious issues. While you may not like your daughter's "weird" way of dressing, she's a responsible young woman who is doing what she needs to do to make a successful transition to adulthood.

* * *

For some girls, one way to fit in with their peers, and possibly drive their parents crazy at the same time, is to dress as differently from their parents as possible. Have you ever noticed teens at the mall or on the streets who have gone all out with their weird dress? You know, the ones with the purple spiked hair and the row of body piercings? These kids really want to be noticed, and the best and easiest way they can think of is to use their appearance to stand out in the crowd. And they certainly do! So, by dressing weird, teens can accomplish several things. They fit in with a chosen group of peers, they get noticed, and they declare their separateness and independence from their parents.

Some teens dress weird as a way of reacting to feeling constantly judged by adults. Through their dress, they are telling adults who see them: "You can't tell me who I am going to be." Because teens have not yet fully developed their own identities, they want to at least be able to communicate with their parents and other adults that while they may not know exactly who they are going to become, they are sure that they are not *you*.

You have to allow this process to occur and realize that as much as you don't like it, it is part of normal and healthy development. The best you can do is not to inadvertently push your daughter to wear weird stuff by constantly being "on her case." Sometimes, the more you pressure her to conform, the more she will dig her heels in. Don't be too judgmental, and trust that, like many other fads, this too shall pass.

Hot Tips

☞ While it may seem like your daughter has lost her own identity and is just following the crowd, she has not totally disappeared! She is just trying to *fit in.* One of the best ways to help your daughter maintain her own identity during this time is to encourage and support her in exploring and nurturing her unique talents, interests, and hobbies. And remember that if you model behaviors that represent *your* unique self, your daughter is more likely to do the same.

☞ While your daughter's interest in guys probably doesn't surprise you, you might be worried that all she cares about is boys. Fathers and other adult males can play an important part in helping teenage girls not become "boy crazy" by validating their physical attractiveness, along with their smarts and strengths, so that they are not starving for male approval.

☞ To develop her independence and feelings of self-worth, your daughter needs ever-increasing opportunities to make age-appropriate decisions of her own. Be patient. Give her room to make mistakes and learn from them. But if your daughter has not begun to show signs of increased independence and self-worth by the time she is a high school junior, don't wait. Get some professional help.

☞ Of course your daughter's friends have a lot of influence over her. Fitting in and belonging are *musts* at this time in her life. So, if your daughter's relationships with her friends seem to be more important than anything else, she is normal! Your daughter is learning about the kinds of people she enjoys spending time with, who she can trust, and how to handle conflicts and changes in relationships. It's not that your opinions and perspectives don't matter. You just *don't know it all* anymore. It's not that you can't say anything, just be careful about what you say, when you say it, and how you sound. And don't take it personally when your daughter does not heed your advice!

☞ So your daughter seems to be spending all her time with her boyfriend, in her room, on the phone, or on the computer. Instead of constantly complaining, drum up some competition. If you suggest things that your daughter enjoys doing, she might just squeeze you in. Take an interest in her interests. It won't kill you to try listening to her music.

☞ If you want your daughter to pursue relationships with guys who treat her as an equal, think about your part in it all. Start by asking yourself what your daughter sees the women in her own family doing. Let her know that in spite of what she may see around her, and what the media might portray, it is not *her job* to take care of any man. If your daughter is constantly exposed to women who defer to men, who put their own needs aside, who don't express their real feelings, or who hide their knowledge and opinions because they fear disapproval or abandonment, she too will see herself as a second-class citizen and begin to behave like one.

☞ You can't protect your daughter from the world like you could when she was younger. And, when it is your daughter who is the brunt of cruelty from her peers, it can be very painful for you to see. Listen, be compassionate, and don't minimize or dismiss her hurt. Let her know that no one deserves to be treated cruelly. Help her consider ways she might be able to protect herself.

☞ The media send some very unhealthy messages to adolescent girls. Talk with your daughter about how the media project images of how women "should" look, and how most of these women are too thin and many have eating disorders. Let her know how much you disapprove of how the media portray women. Encourage your daughter to *boycott* magazines that only focus on looks and don't highlight women's brains and talents.

☞ If you think your daughter's clothes are weird, or you simply don't like the way she dresses, keep your cool. How she dresses is one of the ways your daughter has to express her independence from you and explore her emerging identity. Unless her clothing is clearly and unquestionably provocative, or violates the dress code of where she is going, such as her school, church, or work, tread lightly. While it is OK to ask your daughter to *think* about how she is dressing for a particular occasion, don't make a big deal out of it. There are more important battles to fight!

3

Will I Ever Stop Worrying About Her?
The Vulnerabilities of Adolescent Girls

Some of my friends have older kids, but until now I never really understood what they meant when they said, "Little kids, little problems; big kids, big problems." Now I know! My daughter Tanya is 16, and now that she's so much more independent, I find myself worrying about her a lot more. She's been a reasonably good kid but I'm still afraid she could get into trouble and mess up her life—you know, all the things you hear about: drugs, alcohol abuse, sex, eating disorders, even depression and suicide.

When I read the newspaper or listen to the evening news and hear about all the dangers out there, I feel a wave of panic wash over me. When I was a kid, it seemed like the world was a much safer place. Now it seems like there's danger everywhere.

I think I know Tanya pretty well, but sometimes I'm not sure if she is just going through a stage or if there's really a serious problem brewing. And sometimes I'm not quite sure how to support her through the difficult times and all the stresses. Tanya gets so angry at times, and other times she just withdraws and seems to be really depressed. I get worried about her and I want to help. But sometimes I don't know *how* to help, and after all, it's not like she always welcomes my involvement and advice anyway!

I'm not sure how to handle talking to her about certain topics either, like sex, or drinking, or drugs. I want Tanya to be educated, knowledgeable, and prepared for life, but at the same time I don't want to give her too much information too soon or too fast. For example, my parents couldn't talk to me about sex. I want to be able to talk to my daughter. I want her to see sex as a natural and wonderful part of life. At the same time, especially today, she needs to know the facts and the dangers. But then again, I don't want to give her the wrong message and wind up encouraging her to be sexually active before she's ready. It's really confusing. Yes, I really know now what my friends meant when they said, "Big kids, big problems."—*May, mother of Tanya, age 16*

How do I know if my daughter is in trouble or simply "being a teenager"?
Brielle M.

Sometimes it can be hard to distinguish between "serious" trouble and the normal ups and downs of a teenage girl. Think back to when you were your daughter's age. How would you have let your parents know when something was wrong or you were in trouble? Would you have told them? Would you have shut yourself in your room? Would you have moped around the house? Would you have been irritable and snapped at everyone who crossed your path? Do you see any of these behaviors in your daughter? Watch for signs that her behavior has changed in ways that make you "uncomfortable":

- Is she far more edgy, irritable, and moody than usual?
- Is she more withdrawn, isolated, or "down" than usual?
- Are her eating habits or sleeping patterns changing significantly?
- Is she on the phone or e-mail night and day with her friends and being more secretive about it?
- Is she more easily startled, as if she's hiding something from you and you almost found out?

- Have her grades in school or her behavior in class taken a sudden dive?
- Has she stopped participating in her normal activities, like sports or music lessons?
- Has her network of friends suddenly changed?

One or more of these behavioral changes is a warning sign, an indication that *something* is going on. The best way to find out what's going on with your daughter is to ask: "I'm wondering if something's up. You don't seem like yourself lately. Are you OK?" Asking such a simple question can work so well. Teenage girls are often eager to share their thoughts and feelings if someone only asks them—and if they are reassured that whatever the problem, you are there to help and support them. Remind her that no matter how bad the situation is, the sooner she gets help, the sooner the problem can be resolved. Most teens shut out their parents because they fear the consequences, not because they don't want help.

One warning: If you question your daughter in a critical tone of voice, or if you sound hysterical, like there is a disaster in the works, your daughter might quickly become defensive or simply shut down. So, try as hard as you can to sound interested, reasonable, and calm. Play act if you must; the idea is to get a dialogue going. For example, a critical barrage like, "I know there is something going on. I can tell when you are hiding things from me. You're always getting into trouble. What's wrong with you? What happened this time? What is it? I need to know," is bound to get you nowhere fast.

Also remember that you might get the information or "story" piecemeal. You may find out one bit now, another piece later. Be patient. On some level, most teens want their parents to know if they are really in trouble so they can get the help they need. You need to make it as safe and easy as possible for your daughter to talk to you.

* * *

Many parents wonder if they are underreacting or overreacting to their daughter's moods or behavior. When it really feels like trouble might be brewing, one of the things that can help bring clarity is talking with some of the parents of your daughter's friends. Sometimes this can help you decide if the situation requires your attention. Without other parents to talk with, you have absolutely no frame of reference.

It can also help to connect with other parents when your daughter comes to you and tells you, "All the other kids are allowed to do that." Your daughter certainly uses *her* friends to compare notes about how reasonable or unreasonable your rules and limits are. But too often parents are afraid to compare notes with other parents! It makes no sense for you to exist in total isolation from other parents when you have questions, concerns, or doubts about what is normal or what is trouble. When in doubt, pick up the phone and call the parents of your daughter's friends or other adults whose advice and perspective you value. Establishing and maintaining ongoing contact with other parents will not only help you and them to know what is going on but will also give you someone to talk to when you feel stressed.

* * *

The best way to judge whether your daughter is in trouble is to look at how she is functioning in the different parts of her life. Is she performing as well academically as she has done in the past? Is she involved socially with other teenagers who act in appropriate and respectful ways? While she may be moody at times, are there also times when she is cheerful and reasonable? If your answers are yes, then you probably don't need to be overly concerned. Being a teenager means moving from being a dependent child to becoming an independent adult. Of course, this process is not usually a smooth one; in fact, it is usually full of turmoil. Many times, your daughter will act like a child inside a young woman's body. Sometimes she will act like a 4-year-old; other times she will act like a 24-year-old! But if her overall level of functioning in school, with friends, and with the family has not deteriorated significantly, then you probably don't need to be too worried.

How can parents best support their adolescent daughter through the pressure to experiment with drugs, sex, and shoplifting? *Paige G.*

You know all too well that no matter how hard you try to protect her, your daughter is going to be confronted with temptations involving drugs, sex, and stealing. While talking with your daughter about the importance of her choices is certainly something you need to do, by the time she reaches her teen years, most of her behavior will be determined by the foundation you have already built.

Your daughter has watched and continues to watch what *you* do. Actions speak louder than words. Think about how she sees you dealing with medications, drugs and alcohol, your own sexuality, and issues of honesty. While what you *do* does not guarantee that your daughter will respond in the same way, you are one of her most important role models. If she sees you guided by your own internal compass (as opposed to being largely influenced by external forces), you become a very solid, effective role model for her to resist the pressures and temptations she will encounter.

But, even if you are a good role model for your daughter, you may not be able to prevent her from experimenting with drugs, sex, alcohol, or shoplifting. In addition, she probably has at least some peers who are experimenting in these areas.

It is normal for teens to want to learn from their own experiences, risky though they may be. If your daughter generally shows good judgment, then in all probability her experimentation with risky behaviors is not likely to lead to a dependency or cause other serious or long-term problems for her. But if your daughter generally has poor judgment when it comes to these kinds of issues, you have more reason to be concerned. If you feel that you have no influence on her and that her experimentation is more serious than normal adolescent risk taking, then you need to go to the next step.

Think about getting professional help for you and your daughter. While there are many different approaches to helping a teen in trouble, like supportive counseling on the one end and "Tough Love" support groups on the other end, it is important to get a professional evaluation before deciding on which path to take. A professional can help determine if there are underlying issues that need to be addressed beyond the problem behavior. A professional can also help you and your daughter to learn better communication, which is essential in managing this challenging time.

* * *

Have you ever heard the saying "Prevention is the best medicine?" Well, it's particularly true when it comes to trying to ensure that your daughter is able to resist the pressures of drugs, sex, and shoplifting. To start with, talk with your daughter about these things *now*, even if there is no hint of any problem whatsoever. But one conversation is not enough— the dialogue needs to *continue*. Some parents who have already discussed drugs, sex, and shoplifting with their kids during the calmer preteen years have assumed that this will be enough of an insurance policy. Wrong! The conversations need to continue, especially because even a calm and reasonable preadolescent can become a more difficult, challenging, and turbulent teenager. So, start early, keep talking, and tell her the truth.

* * *

To support your daughter through the pressures to experiment with drugs, sex, and shoplifting, you need to be informed. Most communities have drug information and parenting classes available. Check your local library, school, or community center to see what resources your community offers. Although it might surprise you, many hospitals and clinics also offer courses and workshops that focus on prevention and healthy lifestyles.

In addition, many teen girls find it helpful to be part of youth groups or support groups that can help them band together to resist these pressures. And if you start early enough, your daughter is more likely to find other like-minded kids to hang out with, which might help her to be less vulnerable to peer pressure later on.

For example, some communities support teens in signing "virginity contracts." Other contracts can include abstinence from using drugs or commitments to stay alcohol free. The important component of any of these contracts is having the support of a peer group to resist pressures.

How can we help adolescent girls have a realistic acceptance of their body image? How can we help them through issues of eating disorders? *Andrea W.*

In our society, many, many girls struggle with their feelings about their bodies. While different cultures have different views of what is attractive, each culture has an ideal image of how a woman should look, and every girl measures herself by some standard. For a teenage girl, learning to be realistic and accepting of her body often creates a conflict between what she really looks like and the images portrayed on TV, in the movies, and in teen and women's magazines. Is it any wonder that so many girls develop and struggle with eating disorders?

The most important thing you can do is to consistently communicate to your daughter that what is on the *inside* is what really counts and that her qualities as a person are far more important than her looks. But don't lie to her: You both know that in our society, physical appearance is one of the ways in which people achieve status. It may be *unfair*, but the reality is that some boys choose their girlfriends based only on physical appearance. Be sure to emphasize to your daughter, though, that physical appearance is not the way that *all* guys pick their girlfriends and not the only way in which she will be judged. Her other qualities are important as well.

Don't try to fool your daughter. She knows what she looks like, and you can't sugarcoat it without lying to her. If you think she is a bit overweight, for example, and she asks you about it, be truthful. You should, of course, still emphasize her good qualities, and you can certainly communicate that you love her for who she is, not how she looks. But if you try to tell your daughter she is thin, when she knows she is 20 pounds overweight, she will know you are not being truthful and will not be able to trust your feedback in the future.

Here are some highlights of the things that you should be sure to communicate to your daughter:

- How she feels about herself is more important than her physical appearance. A girl who feels good about herself comes across as more attractive than other girls who might have better physical features but who don't feel good about themselves.
- Even if a girl does not have exceptional natural beauty, she can still take good care of herself with a healthy diet and a moderate amount of exercise.
- "Different strokes for different folks": What one person sees as attractive is not necessarily what another person would regard as beautiful. Images of beauty vary from culture to culture and from person to person.

- The vast majority of teenage girls are uncomfortable with their bodies. What you would regard as a minor flaw may seem like a major disaster to your teenage daughter. As her body is changing, your daughter may lack confidence in her appearance and exaggerate her imperfections.

You should also ask yourself: "What am I modeling for my daughter in terms of how I relate to *my* own body and what does she hear *me* saying about the bodies of others?" Parents who model a good balance between taking care of their bodies, while not being obsessive about it, and those who speak respectfully about the bodies of others (no matter what their size and shape) are doing the best possible job of helping their daughters to accept their own bodies.

* * *

There is a "body awareness" exercise that is fun and might help your daughter develop a more realistic acceptance of her body. It is called *body building*. And you and your daughter can do this together. Assign a value to each body part: for example, naturally straight teeth may cost $10; straight teeth with braces may cost only $5. Each of you should "construct" your ideal body (eyes, nose, mouth, hair, etc.) by "buying" various features, but you each have only $100 to spend.

This exercise can help your daughter think about her priorities and her concerns with her own body. Then talk with her about the body she has "designed" and share your design with her. Use this as a point of departure to talk about her physical appearance, her projected image to others, and how she thinks others view her. Explain to her why you chose certain features and what your priorities are. Talk to her about what you have learned about yourself by doing this exercise. Encourage her to share her thoughts and ideas with you.

You might try doing this exercise a couple of times each year. Save your body designs in a book, so you can look back on them and see how your ideas have changed over time. This can be an especially powerful exercise as your daughter's body is changing and developing so much during this time.

How can we help our daughter welcome and appreciate her sexuality and stay in charge of it? *Kelly Z.*

As your daughter approaches puberty, she will be confronting major changes in her body and her physical appearance. Some girls adjust to these changes more easily than others. While you cannot control when these changes happen or control your daughter's feelings about them, you can certainly set the stage for her to welcome and appreciate her developing body and sexuality.

One of the most important things that parents can do is learn how to talk to their daughters (and their sons, for that matter) about sex and sexuality.

However, for many parents, this is very difficult, especially since many of their own parents considered such discussions taboo. In spite of the difficulty, it is very important that you try to be open to discussing sexual and gender-related issues with your daughter. She is probably learning about sex and the facts of life in her health class in school, and she is surely talking about it with her girlfriends. But that is not enough: It is part of the responsibility of being a parent to have open discussions about sex with your daughter. It is best to start these discussions when your daughter is a preadolescent, and then you can continue on a more sophisticated level as she matures. It is OK to tell your daughter your own feelings about sex and relationships. Remember that she is watching you to see how you deal with your own sexuality.

Be sure that you talk to your daughter about sexuality as an extension of who she is. Accepting her sexuality is easier when she feels positive about her appearance, her personality, and her self-worth. Be reassured that girls who tend to use good judgment and are "in charge" of other parts of their lives are likely to use good judgment and be in charge of their sexuality as well.

Although it might be difficult or almost impossible to think about it right now, most parents want their daughters to grow up to have a satisfying sexual relationship. You can and should acknowledge this openly to your daughter. At the same time, you must also express your concerns: that she could choose the wrong person to be sexual with, that she could become pregnant, or that she could get an STD. As you continue to talk to your daughter about accepting and appreciating her sexuality, stress the importance of her using good judgment in the choices she makes.

* * *

In spite of all you might do, your daughter may have significant difficulty with welcoming and appreciating her sexuality. Some girls are so afraid of their emerging sexuality that they starve themselves to a point of stopping their physical development. These girls have discovered that when they don't eat, and are seriously undernourished, they no longer menstruate. Thus, they can remain children—in other words, nonsexual. Other girls are overwhelmed with sexual feelings and have not learned self-control. They can't say no to sexual activity, might become promiscuous at an early age, and eventually sacrifice a great deal of their self-esteem to their impulsive sexual needs and desires. Furthermore, these girls often develop a bad reputation as a "slut" or a "whore," which ultimately damages their self-esteem further since such reputations are hard to shake. If your daughter seems to be moving toward either of these extremes or already falls into one of these categories, professional help is definitely indicated. Talk to her doctor, guidance counselor, or clergy to find the right person to help her.

* * *

Girls who are lesbians or bisexual struggle with their developing sexuality because their sexual feelings are not developing along "standard" lines. These girls are healthy, normal, and well adjusted, but they fear that the differences in their sexual orientation will not be accepted by their families, friends, or society as a whole. Because our society is predominantly heterosexual, many of these girls have a hard time accepting their sexual orientation since it doesn't fit "the norm." Teenagers in general have a hard time not fitting into the norm, so an issue as sensitive and crucial as sexual orientation is especially difficult.

Some teen girls go through a stage of experimentation and need to be accepted and supported during this phase of exploring their sexual orientation. These girls might declare themselves lesbians, bisexual, or heterosexual at different times. Other girls are firm and unchanging in their knowledge that they are lesbians or bisexual and need to feel fully accepted for who they are inside.

Regardless of whether it is temporary experimentation or a lasting part of her identity, if your daughter thinks that she is a lesbian or is bisexual, *she needs your support*. While at first you may be shocked, or even horrified, especially if you had no clue about her emerging sexual orientation, you've got to put your negative reaction aside and be there for her. This is a hard time for her, and she needs you. And, slowly but surely, you will come to realize that your daughter is not abnormal, immoral, or perverted. She is the same daughter you have loved and admired all along. The more you talk with her, the more you will learn and the more you will be able to help her develop into a mature and happy woman.

If you are really unable to overcome your prejudices, or if your daughter cannot accept her own sexual orientation, there are numerous gay and lesbian groups that can be of help. If you live in a large city, there are probably parent support groups as well as teen support groups. Don't be afraid that by attending such a group you will *make* your daughter a lesbian if she isn't! There are also a number of national organizations that support gay, lesbian, and bisexual lifestyles. Many of these organizations have Web sites as well. These resources can go a long way toward comforting a teen (and her parents) who may feel alienated, confused, or rejected.

Some people believe that anyone who chooses to be gay or bisexual could just as easily choose to be heterosexual. This is simply not true. While some girls are, in fact, choosing and experimenting with sexual lifestyles, for many girls their sexual orientation is not a *choice* but a fact of their lives. They cannot choose to be otherwise.

Whether if by biology or by choice your daughter is a lesbian or is bisexual, she needs to welcome and appreciate her sexual orientation, and be in charge of it, just as much as her heterosexual peers. And your acceptance of her can be the *most important* factor in her achieving a healthy adjustment to all aspects of her sexuality.

In what ways does our society tell girls that it is not all right for them to express anger? In what ways can we help them express outrage or anger in healthy ways? *Rachel R.*

In general, our society is more accepting of aggression in males than in females. Girls are expected to control their anger more than boys. They are taught that the expression of angry emotions, especially in public, is not appropriate or "ladylike." Instead of showing their anger, girls are taught to manipulate and use their "charms" to get their way. Numerous examples of this can be seen on TV and in the movies, where females are depicted as sneaking, plotting, or using their wiles to gain the upper hand. The fact is that neither the aggressive behavior allowed in boys nor the manipulative behavior encouraged in girls is a healthy way to express anger.

Your daughter needs to learn how to express all of her feelings (including her anger) *assertively* but not aggressively. She needs to learn how to demonstrate her anger without being physically or verbally hurtful, to be direct and forthright without being manipulative, and to ask for what she wants and needs. As her parent, you can teach your daughter to talk about her feelings openly and help her explore how to deal with them.

Because anger is often difficult for girls to express, your daughter needs your ideas and feedback about how to communicate her angry feelings. You can give her some examples from your own life—like how you assertively let a boss or friend know that you were angry with him or her and how you eventually resolved the issue. In addition, how you express your anger directly to your daughter can also serve to model healthy ways of communicating angry feelings. Remember, if you do not allow your daughter to express her anger directly, the long-term consequences can be quite negative, including chronic frustration, depression, and stress.

* * *

Some girls cannot even identify when they feel angry, and so they can't express their anger in healthy ways. Whether you realize it or not, over time you have learned how to "name" your feelings. Some kids need help simply in finding words to identify *what* they are feeling. If your daughter says she never gets angry, you should know that this is simply not possible: The problem might be that she never learned to identify or label this feeling.

If your daughter never identifies herself as feeling angry, help her. You can do this by simply labeling her anger for her: When she pouts and gets sullen, snippy, or bitchy, suggest to her that she might be angry. When she goes to her room, shuts the door, and blasts her music, suggest to her that she might be angry. When she withdraws, won't talk to you, or gives you that glaring look, eye roll, and cold shoulder, again, suggest to her that she might be angry. Even if you are wrong, asking your daughter to identify her feelings more carefully will help her clarify what *is* anger and what is *not* anger. This process will help your daughter to differentiate among her various emotions.

For other girls, the problem is not identifying their angry feelings, but finding acceptable ways of *showing* their anger. Ask your daughter to think about someone she has met who seems to be able to show her anger in reasonable and appropriate ways. Then ask your daughter to think about someone who she would describe as never getting angry. Explain that what she is really describing is someone who has learned to stuff her anger, to hide it very cleverly, and to appear as if she is simply never angry. After all, nobody *never* gets angry. While one person shows anger and the other doesn't, point out that both people *have* angry feelings, but one of them has not found a way to show or express anger.

Adolescent girls who cannot identify their angry feelings or who fear having normal feelings of anger often engage in self-destructive behaviors to communicate their hidden anger. When angry feelings are not expressed, tension builds inside, and eventually the pressure needs an escape. Some girls find this escape in extreme behaviors, like cutting themselves with a sharp object. This self-mutilation is almost always a sign of unidentified or unexpressed anger. And it is obviously very dangerous. While your daughter may not be engaging in such an extreme behavior, be on the lookout if she doesn't ever seem to be able to show her anger. Anger is a necessary and healthy emotion.

Remember that if there is no acceptable way for your daughter to express her anger—if she is never allowed to yell, stomp off, or even slam a door—then you are inadvertently forming a blockade and her anger will eat away inside her. Unfortunately, many parents punish their kids for healthy expressions of anger. And unfortunately, many parents still believe that they have the right to express their own anger but their children don't. Take a look at your behavior and focus on making whatever changes are needed so that your daughter can identify and express her anger in healthy, nonharmful ways. Although slamming doors and stomping feet are unpleasant, they are not harmful and may for now be considered a developmentally normal behavior. Over time, your daughter will develop more mature ways of expressing her anger.

What are the factors that lead teenage girls to engage in premarital sex? *Taylor K.*

It would certainly make you, as a parent, feel more secure and more in control if you knew the factors that led to a number of risk-taking behaviors, including premarital sex. However, while researchers continue to learn more and more about the characteristics and environmental factors that lead to adolescent risk-taking behaviors, we have yet to come up with a clear and concise list of proven factors. What we do know is that certain combinations of factors seem to make teen girls more vulnerable to having premarital sex.

Here are some of the major factors that have been shown to contribute to teenage girls engaging in premarital sex:

- *Peer pressure*: Peer pressure is a very powerful force, and when a guy gives your daughter the message that "everybody does it" and it is what she is expected to do if she "loves him," the pressure is enormous. Add to this the possibility that her peer group of female friends is also engaging in premarital sex, and you can imagine how hard it would be for her to say "no." The old stereotype of the boys bragging in the locker room about their sexual conquests is no longer limited to just the guys. It is not unusual nowadays for girls as well as guys to brag about their sexual experimentation.
- *Drug and alcohol use*: While drug and alcohol use do not automatically lead to premarital sex, they do reduce inhibitions and cloud judgment. Girls who are working hard to manage their normal sexual feelings and attractions often find themselves breaking their own rules and "going further" sexually when they are under the influence of drugs or alcohol.

- *Distant or nonexistent relationships with family, especially fathers*: Girls who don't feel connected with anyone in their family and who feel no one has time for them or much interest in their struggles often look for love and acceptance through premarital sex. This is particularly true for girls who have a distant or nonexistent relationship with their fathers. A father is a girl's first admirer, and this relationship forms the foundation on which her self-esteem as a woman is built. Without this foundation, many teen girls develop an addiction to male attention that then leads to premarital sex.

- *Lack of friendship group*: Girls who feel isolated, rejected, and unconnected to a group of female friends often look for other ways to bond and feel like they belong. These are the girls who often fool themselves into thinking that engaging in a sexual encounter with a guy is a substitute for a relationship. They are looking for a quick fix that will make them feel like a "somebody" instead of a "nobody."

- *Early exposure to sexual images*: In our culture today, kids are exposed to highly provocative, sexual imagery at a very young age. Romance and sexuality are even marketed to preschoolers! Well before they are old enough to understand and integrate the complex factors that are involved, kids are bombarded with pictures and products that lead them to a premature and false "maturity" about sex. It is no wonder, then, that premarital sex is now so widely "accepted," even for girls as young as 13 or 14.

- *Media portrayals of teen sex:* Media examples of teen sex are rampant and fill the TV and movie screens. Magazines, even those targeted to young teens, often include articles with instructions on sexual techniques! Even those media images that depict the struggles or problems caused by premarital teen sex often have sensational, glamorous heroines. Adolescent girls often want to imitate the clothes, hair, makeup, *and sexual activity* of their "heroines."

While you cannot raise your daughter in a bubble and protect her from all of these influences, your conscious awareness and attention to these factors can help you in talking with her and building her strength, resolve, and resiliency.

* * *

One of the results of the increasing number of single-parent families is that more and more teens are exposed to their parents meeting and becoming involved with other adults in a sexual or romantic way. Years ago, most teens heard only about how their parents met and became involved with one another. Today, many teens from divorced families witness the development of a sexual relationship firsthand as they see a parent meet a new partner, date, and develop a sexual relationship. Sometimes teens even share dating stories with their parents! Single parents are often in a very difficult position. They want to balance their normal and healthy desire for a relationship, including sex, with a message to their daughters that sex should be reserved for marriage, or at least for serious and mature relationships when they are older.

Most adolescent girls who live in single-parent families live with their mothers and therefore have an opportunity to closely observe their mother's dating behavior. It is important for a single mother to think about how she behaves sexually with a man in front of her daughter. Does her daughter see one, long-term serious relationship or a series of brief encounters? Does her daughter observe her acting or dressing in provocative or seductive ways to get male attention? Does her daughter see that a sexual relationship is part of a deeper commitment or only a form of temporary entertainment?

While most adolescent girls from divorced families live with their mothers, their father's dating and sexual relationships can also have a powerful impact on them. Adolescent girls who see their father's pursuit of women as significantly more important than spending time with them are more likely to engage in premarital sex. A divorced father needs to spend time with his daughter one-on-one. He needs to be sensitive to his daughter's need for attention and validation and not always include his girlfriend, or even new wife, when he spends time with his daughter.

Single parents who date and develop meaningful sexual relationships with new partners can have a positive influence on their daughter's developing sexuality. They can accomplish this by being attentive to when and how they introduce their daughters to their new relationships, especially sexual relationships. Although single parents certainly deserve to develop new sexual relationships, they also need to carefully consider how their behavior will affect their adolescent daughters, particularly the messages they may be sending about sex outside of marriage. They must be prepared to be confronted by their daughters about whether or not they are practicing what they preach.

How common is drug abuse among adolescent girls? Is marijuana something that will be harmful in the long term?
Lauren V.

The organizations that monitor drug usage in the United States have been reporting a steady increase in drug use among adolescent girls. Adolescent girls are using more illicit drugs now than they were in the past. The data reflect two very troubling trends: (a) girls are using more "gateway" drugs than in prior years (gateway drugs are drugs that "open the gates" to more dangerous drug use), including alcohol, cigarettes, and marijuana; and (b) girls are using more appetite-suppressant drugs (both over the counter and illicit).

Because most teenagers believe that they are invincible, they think that they can use drugs and the drugs will not harm them. The fact is, they are not totally wrong. Most teens who have experimented with marijuana or alcohol, or even other drugs, have not been significantly harmed in either the short or the long run. Most often, it is the teens who are *abusing* drugs (the long-term and frequent users), not those who are briefly experimenting, that experience long-term negative effects. However, there are occasionally dramatic news stories about kids who have tried a drug just once, gotten severely injured, had an extremely negative reaction, or even died. So no matter which way you look at it, there *is* a risk.

Even marijuana, which is certainly less dangerous than many other drugs, has risks associated with it. For example, recent studies have shown that there have been cases of men and women in their 30s and 40s, with no other predisposing factors, having serious heart attacks following marijuana use. In addition, researchers continue to look at how marijuana might contribute to infertility and addictions. Diet drugs have been shown to have very serious metabolic consequences. And there are always new "designer drugs" that have unknown consequences.

The bottom line is that drug abuse among adolescent girls is on the increase and that new risks continue to emerge. So, you should make sure your daughter is well aware of the consequences of drug use.

* * *

One of the problems we face in trying to address the issue of drug abuse today is that the kinds of drugs that are available to teens are constantly changing. Drugs that did not even exist a year ago quickly become the drug of choice. This constantly changing drug scene makes it extremely difficult to determine how common the use of a particular drug is among adolescent girls. And in fact, when a teen girl decides to use a drug, she often doesn't even know what she has taken.

The bottom line is that we simply have no way of knowing or predicting what the long-term effects of these new designer drugs will be.

What causes depression in adolescent girls? Is depression common among teenage girls? *Brenda S.*

There have been many studies about the causes of depression in adolescent girls, and the conclusion is that depression is caused by a number of different factors that act together. This is called the biopsychosocial model of depression.

The "bio" part of the word *biopsychosocial* refers to the biological or physical causes of depression. Scientists believe that there is a genetic link to depression, which means that if there is depression in your family, your daughter may be more likely to have it herself. Besides genes, your internal chemistry plays a big role in depression. Neurotransmitters and hormones are two kinds of chemicals in the brain that can cause a problem if they are either overactive or underactive. When chemistry is the major factor, we sometimes refer to the person as having a "chemical imbalance." Teenagers' hormones are in a state of rapid change, and their mood swings are a direct result of these biological changes. Sometimes these changes are so extreme that they cause an imbalance that can result in depression.

The "psycho" part of the word *biopsychosocial* refers to the psychological aspects of depression. This includes thoughts, beliefs, and feelings about oneself, other people, and life in general. When thoughts, feelings, or beliefs are negative too frequently, depression can result. Some examples of psychological variables that might contribute to depression in teenage girls include feelings of low self-esteem, a sense of powerlessness, a negative self-image, a poor body image, unrealistic expectations that lead to repeated disappointments, and pessimistic thinking.

Finally, the "social" part of the word *biopsychosocial* is important to consider because kids don't grow up in a vacuum. Social refers to the external environment: family, peers, the community you live in, and the culture at large, including things like media and music. Think of all the things that can be troubling to your daughter in these areas. Relationship difficulties, family conflicts, problems in school, fitting in socially, and confusing or depressing images in the media only begin the list!

Given that depression is so complex and can have so many causes, the odds are pretty high that your teenage daughter will go through some normal "depression" as she goes through this challenge-filled period in her development. However, there are some important warning signs to watch out for because they may signal that her depression is more serious than just "normal teenage moodiness." Look for significant changes in your daughter's behavior:

- If she loses interest in things, especially things that she used to enjoy
- If she begins to withdraw or isolate herself
- If there is a significant drop in her performance in school and it seems as if she no longer cares
- If she experiences a prolonged period in which she seems "down"
- If she starts to act out and take more risks than usual
- If she has more than the usual number of headaches, stomachaches, or colds
- If she seems especially fatigued
- If she is particularly irritable or agitated
- If she has more difficulty concentrating
- If she feels worthless or has thoughts of death or suicide
- If there are changes in her usual sleeping or eating patterns (either an increase or decrease)

If your daughter shows two or more of these symptoms for more than a couple of weeks, get a professional evaluation. If she talks to you or anyone else about death or suicide, even if she later says she was "only kidding," don't wait: Get help immediately.

How much awareness do adolescent girls have of the destructive violence in relationships (like date rape)? Are girls today being sufficiently educated to protect themselves from harm? How can I teach personal safety? *Eva B.*

Given the diversity of personal experiences with family, peers, community, and the media, it stands to reason that the extent to which adolescent girls are aware of the potential dangers in relationships varies a great deal. Some teenage girls are quite naive, whereas others are more street smart and savvy than the average adult.

Schools are increasingly offering violence prevention programs to their students, many of which provide information about date rape. Small workshop-type programs, that teach students skills and attitudes that they can use to avoid or effectively respond to potentially dangerous situations, seem to be the most successful. You should familiarize yourself with what your daughter's school is doing to teach her how to protect herself against violent acts such as date rape. Try to participate in violence prevention programs and curriculum development through parent groups such as the PTA; work to ensure that personal safety strategies are taught at your daughter's school.

It can help both you *and* your daughter to know some of the facts about date rape:

- Children who were exposed to verbal, emotional, physical, or sexual abuse early on may be at greater risk for being victimized by date rape.
- Girls with low self-esteem and poor communication skills may also be at greater risk.
- The use of drugs or alcohol is often associated with date rape.
- Strategies associated with rape avoidance include verbal resistance, physical resistance, and fleeing.

As always, a good open relationship with your daughter can help a lot. If you are comfortable talking with her about difficult topics like violence and date rape, you'll be better able to help her

- make good judgments about peers and boys
- be more aware of how she presents herself
- become a clear communicator
- be cognizant of the dangers of getting drunk or high
- make an emergency plan should she need one

As a final note, it is important to remember that date rape is the exception rather than the rule. While your concerns about your daughter's safety are natural, always remember to instill realistic and positive expectations of relationships for her as well.

* * *

Most high schools now have personal safety classes or include violence prevention programs as part of their health curriculum. This is an excellent way to begin the process of educating adolescent girls on how to protect themselves, but it is only a first step. Too many teenage girls have experiences in which they are coerced into a sexual activity that they are not sure they want to be part of. Sometimes the coercion is verbal, sometimes it includes the threat of physical violence, sometimes there is actual physical force or violence, and sometimes a girl's submission is achieved by the use of a drug or substance given surreptitiously (a drug secretly dropped into her drink, for example).

Many parents are angry and upset and want to know why this continues to occur despite the programs offered in school. There are two contributing factors that might explain this. The first factor is that many adolescent girls want desperately to fit in, so they let their guard down in order to be part of a group and be accepted. In spite of what they have learned, they make foolish choices and may disregard their personal safety to be accepted and belong to the group. The second factor is that far too many parents do not adequately address violence prevention at home. Even if violence prevention is being addressed in your daughter's school, this does not mean that there is no need for parents to talk about it! On the contrary! Home is the most critical location for teaching values. And personal safety can be taught best by parents who are willing to speak about it openly in a caring, supportive fashion. Tell your daughter that you care enough about her to want her not to get hurt. Talk to her about making wise choices about whom she spends her time with; talk to her about not putting herself into risky situations. Work out an "emergency" plan, which should include carrying enough money to get home from wherever she is.

Think about contacting your local police station to inquire about any special resources or violence prevention activities in your community. There are some excellent programs that teach techniques of personal safety and how to cope with the threat of violence. You can encourage your daughter to take classes like karate or kick boxing, where she will not only learn self-defense techniques but where she will become more empowered by her physical capabilities.

How can I help my daughter judge how to have a good time with her peers and not abuse drugs at the same time? *Tom F.*

As you know, judgment is something that develops with maturity—but you can do a number of things to help. Having a good, solid, open relationship with your daughter, preferably one that was established early on, is the key here. Talk to your daughter about drugs. Create an atmosphere in which you can talk frequently and openly. Get into relaxed discussions with her about her own attitudes about drugs and about those of her peers. Asking rather than telling is often the most productive route; lecturing your daughter does not generally translate into good communication. You may say all the right things, but if it goes in one ear and out the other you've accomplished nothing. Listen closely, but resist the temptation to chime in with your own reactions and judgments. Be prepared for her questions: She might ask you about your own history of drug use. Decide in advance how you want to handle such sensitive questions: She is likely to know if you are fudging the truth. Do let her know that she can rely on you to help without fear of punishment if she should have a question or a problem.

If you've done your homework and laid the groundwork with a history of open and honest discussions, it's now time to give her credit for her own sensibilities. It sends the signal that you trust her instincts and decisions, which is an empowering message and a boost to her esteem. If your daughter has a healthy sense of her own power and feels good about herself, she will be able to stand her own ground with peers. In many cases, parents are pleasantly surprised at the wisdom and inner resources that their teenage daughters show.

* * *

This might surprise you, but some research has shown that the single most common location for drug use among adolescents with a drug problem is in their own bedroom with a small group of friends! What this means is that you need to know what your daughter is doing—even when she is "safe at home." Parents should use the "who, what, when, where, and how" method of communicating to help their teenagers avoid drug use. Know *who* your daughter is hanging out with. If she is with others who have a drug abuse history, your daughter is very likely to be sucked in and tempted. Know *what* she is doing when she goes out with her friends. Know *when* she is leaving and when she will be home. Give her a reasonable curfew. Be sure she tells you *where* she will be. Get a phone number where you can reach her, especially if she is with someone you do not know well. And find out *how* her activities were. Speak with her afterward to find out if she had a good time. Don't pry, and don't expect to know all the details, but make it clear that you are available to discuss what was fun as well as what, if anything, went wrong. By asking these questions you help set clear standards for acceptable behaviors. Through discussion, you help form a stronger bond with your daughter. One of the most protective factors against drug use by adolescents is a strong family bond.

What are some effective ways of helping adolescent girls cope with anxiety and depression? Is there a list of methods that are practical and applicable? *Miranda L.*

There are three important steps you can take to help your daughter cope with anxiety and depression. Step one: Use every available opportunity to help your daughter develop her inner resources, so that her coping skills will be in place when she needs them most. Step two: Help your daughter to identify her problems clearly and practically, rather than just reacting to them emotionally. Step three: Help empower your daughter to resolve her problems in a realistic, constructive, and hopeful fashion. Here are the details for these three steps.

Step 1: Developing Inner Resources

Don't wait for a problem to arise to try and teach your daughter coping skills, because once a problem arises, she may be too emotional and upset to start to learn any new skills. You can help her learn good coping skills all the rest of the time, however, by using every calm opportunity to help her "build her resources." "Resources" for an adolescent girl include a healthy sense of self-esteem and confidence, the ability to be assertive, an understanding of the relationship between her own actions and choices and their consequences, and the ability to soothe herself when she's upset.

Ways in which you can help your daughter develop her resources include the following:

- role modeling effective behaviors and strategies
- providing opportunities for appropriate and open self-expression
- offering adequate stimulation and challenge
- ensuring avenues for tension release
- allowing for ample opportunity to interact with other teens
- listening carefully and guiding rather than preaching and lecturing
- validating your daughter's perspective
- encouraging and facilitating problem solving
- communicating confidence in your daughter's abilities
- making certain that your daughter feels valued, respected, and trusted

Make sure your daughter knows that even though her self-esteem can feel shaky at times (and this is certainly a typical adolescent experience), you know she has good resources. When things go astray, and she says she doesn't have any resources or skills (as so frequently occurs when a teen is having a problem and feeling too anxious or depressed to think clearly), remind her about things like

- the last time she helped a friend out of a jam
- how she thought the world would come to an end when she didn't make the team or get a good grade but was able to recover and turn things around

- when she came out on top in some activity or situation
- how many friends rely on her for her compassion, understanding, and problem-solving skills
- how she has found ways to make herself feel better in the past, through exercise, listening to music, or talking to friends

These are some of the ways you can help her to identify her strengths, assets, and accomplishments and remind her of her effective coping skills.

Step 2: Identifying Problems Clearly and Practically

If you believe your daughter is experiencing anxiety or depression, try to determine where it's coming from. The source of her anxiety or depression can be *internal or external*, and frequently it is a combination of both.

Internal sources of distress can be psychological or physical.

- Psychological sources of anxiety and depression include thoughts and feelings that are dysfunctional or irrational (i.e., unrealistic expectations, excessive self-criticism, overexaggeration or dramatizing, or making everything seem like a catastrophe).
- Physical sources of anxiety and depression refer to feelings of anxiety or depression that seem to come from within but do not seem to be linked to her

way of thinking. Physical sources include surges in hormones that typically occur during adolescence, a chemical imbalance, or a genetic history of anxiety disorders or depression (when anxiety or depression "runs in the family").

External sources of distress include stress related to family conflicts, peer pressure, school worries, and concerns about the world in general.

To further complicate things, anxiety and depression usually stem from a combination of these factors. By listening carefully to your daughter, you can help her to understand exactly what is troubling her and help her clarify the source of the problem.

Step 3: Generating a Realistic Problem-Solving Plan

Once you've helped your daughter to understand what the problem is, it's time to guide her in constructing a clear, practical plan on how to handle it. Note the word *guide*. It's important to let *her* be the one to work out the details of the plan. In this way, you communicate to her that you believe in the strength of her own resources and in her ability to handle the problem. This is not to say you can't help. You should be available but not intrusive—quite a challenge during this age of increasing independence!

Instead of offering advice and instructions to your daughter, ask questions, offer suggestions, and let her make the final choices. Be patient. Teens need to feel that they are in control, even when they are not! Be optimistic and encouraging. Tell her that there is always the hope of finding a positive resolution, even though it may not be easy to find. Send the message that experiencing frustration and failure is a natural part of eventual success. Remind her to identify and use other support systems for help: her network of friends, a church group, members of the extended family, a favorite coach or teacher. Help your daughter to be forgiving, to adjust her expectations of herself and others (even of you!), and to do something nice and soothing for herself when she's upset. In other words, help her learn to take good care of herself.

Remember, some anxiety and depression are normal during adolescence. There are many challenges and many disappointments. Your daughter needs to know that it is normal to feel anxious and depressed sometimes. Your daughter's anxiety or depression may be serious, though, if it results in significant changes in her behavior, if it gets in the way of her usual social and recreational activities, or if it results in persistent problems in school or at home. If you believe that your daughter is more than mildly anxious or depressed, seek professional counseling.

What are the scars we are leaving on our adolescent girls having divorced their fathers when they were in elementary school? How can we best help them mend?
Stephanie P.

While a divorce is certainly traumatic for everyone in the family, research has shown that it is the ongoing conflict and fighting between parents, divorced or not, that is most damaging to children. Divorce produces feelings of loss, sadness, and often anger; but the divorce itself does not necessarily produce permanent scars. It is the amount of time a child has been exposed to conflict—during the marriage, during the separation and divorce, and during the post-divorce years—that is most highly related to a child's adjustment. Divorced parents who actively and cooperatively work at co-parenting, who let go of old hurts and put their children's needs first, can and often have happy, well-adjusted children.

Perhaps the most obvious scar that divorce can leave on an adolescent girl is the elimination of a healthy role model of a male–female relationship at a time when she most needs one. In order for teens to develop healthy expectations of what to look for and how to behave with people of the opposite sex, it is important for them to witness positive and healthy "coupling" behavior, including such things as demonstrations of affection toward one another, compromise, and appropriate conflict resolution. Without the opportunity to see these interactions, they lose a critically important chance to learn how to develop and maintain a healthy relationship.

In our society, it is most often fathers rather than mothers who wind up spending less time with their children following a divorce. As a result, another scar may develop because girls whose parents are divorced often experience their father's departure as a form of personal "abandonment." This can result in feelings of anger and distrust toward males in general. When these feelings are acted on (often unknowingly) in their relationships with boys, and later on with men, problems are likely to follow. Your daughter may won-der: "Can I ever truly rely on a man?" Her views of men as reliable and dependable, and her ability to be intimate and to trust, can all suffer if her father does not remain an active part of her life.

In spite of their parents' efforts to reassure them to the contrary, some children become scarred be-cause they feel personally responsible for their par-ents' divorce. This can leave them with feelings of self-blame, inadequacy, and low self-esteem. Even though these feelings are irrational and unwarranted, many a girl has thought that if only she had done more or been better somehow, her parents would not have divorced! The sense of failure and guilt that can accompany this way of thinking can be very dam-aging.

Some fathers provide a balancing force for their daughters—someone to lean on or talk to when there's tension with their mothers. Without their fathers, these girls do not have the option of turning to someone for a second opinion when they disagree with Mom. Without a father's additional perspective, a girl may be left with fewer resources for making wise decisions and good judgments. In addition, in some families, the father has been the primary disciplinarian. Therefore, his leaving could result in an increase in behavior problems during this period of potential rebellion. This loss of her father as a balancing force in her family can scar a daughter.

In many instances, one of the consequences of a divorce is that a mother who has not worked outside the home, or who has only been working part time, might now need to seek full-time employment. As a result, she may be less available, and her children are less likely to have an adult at home as much as they used to. Without a parent to provide supervision and support, teens can become more vulnerable to engaging in risky behaviors that can leave damaging scars.

While there is no question that a divorce is painful for everyone in the family, there is a great deal you can do to prevent some of the scars from forming and to help the other unavoidable scars to heal.

Mothers: You can help heal some of the scars of divorce by not making any negative references about your ex-husband. You should also be careful not to make negative comments about men in general. Even an inadvertent sarcastic comment about men can be damaging. Scarring is minimized when your daughter has your support to continue to have a good relationship with her father. No matter how *you* may feel, it is critically important that you don't make your daughter feel like she has to choose between you and her dad.

Fathers: No matter how angry you may be, don't bad-mouth your ex-wife and don't make disparaging comments about women. If your daughter lives primarily with her mother, it is critical that you not undermine the rules and limits that your ex-wife may have set. If possible, work together with your ex-wife in setting the boundaries and establishing consistent rules in both houses. As the first important male in your daughter's life, your love and approval have a great deal of power. Therefore, be sure that you do not base your love and approval on your daughter favoring you over her mother.

Mothers and fathers: Make it very clear that your daughter is in *no way* responsible for your divorce. Help your daughter to develop trust in relationships. If you can, expose her to healthy couples that she can use as role models for her own early relationship efforts. Encourage your daughter to develop friendships. You can caution her about precipitous commitments, but don't overdo it. Make yourself available to your daughter. If you're not around much, she'll be less likely to come to you with her concerns and problems. Make an extra effort to truly listen to her perceptions. Reassure your daughter that healing takes time.

While divorce is always difficult, in many cases it is the only viable route. And there may be a possible benefit: Divorce can help empower your daughter by demonstrating that when there are significant problems in a relationship, especially in the case of abusive relationships, there are options. In this way, divorce can emphasize a woman's responsibility for her own choices and demonstrate her ability to control the circumstances of her life.

How does a parent respond to an adolescent who refuses to behave or follow the rules? *Candice B.*

This is the time in your daughter's life when it is normal for her to test the limits. She wants more control over her life and her environment as she takes a giant step toward adulthood. "Testing the limits" and bending (or breaking) your rules is a normal part of her growing up. She is simply trying to establish her own rules and expectations and develop the skills and self-confidence that she will need as an adult. Hence, arguments over things like privacy, curfews, peers, clothes, the phone, school, and the ever-popular messy room seem to be endless. While it is tempting to simply lay down the law as you were probably able to do when she was younger, it is likely that you have discovered that this just doesn't work very well any more. Now, in order to help your daughter develop responsible "adult" attitudes, you need to sit down and talk with her and negotiate what the rules will be. While this will take much longer, your daughter is much more likely to follow rules that have been established through negotiation than those you dictate.

Here are a few pointers to help you with the negotiation process:

- Be sure to communicate to your daughter that you insist on having rules because you love her and are concerned for her well-being, not because you want to control her.

- Emphasize that along with the benefits of living at home come some responsibilities—and, as she gets older, her responsibilities will increase as a part of her growing maturity. If a sense of responsibility was not established earlier in her childhood, your daughter may have a feeling of entitlement by now, which will make any rules very hard to enforce. But don't give up. Be consistent and follow through.

- Remember that negotiation, by definition, is a two-way street. Go into the talks with an idea of what you will be willing to give, not just with a series of expectations of her. For example, "OK, I understand that some concerts run late and I am willing to extend curfew on those occasions; but you in turn must agree to call by 11 p.m."

- Join with your daughter to establish mutually agreed on fair rules and, periodically, review them together. Allow your daughter to have input into the rules and the consequences. While this process may sound tedious (and may even rub you the wrong way entirely), it is far more likely to succeed at this stage of her development than the top-down version of establishing rules.

■ Write down the compromises you reach and post them where you can both see them. This can help later on if one of you "forgets" what you agreed on.

The added benefit of negotiating with your daughter is that she will learn a very important skill that she can take with her into the world as she expands her autonomy.

* * *

While conflicts with your daughter about homework, curfews, and chores are part of parenting an adolescent, there are times when the extent of oppositional and defiant behavior goes beyond what is acceptable and normal. For example, if no matter how fairly you negotiate an agreement, your daughter consistently breaks that agreement, it might be a warning sign of bigger problems. If it seems like your daughter is constantly provoking you or looking for things to fight about, this too can be a sign of more serious problems, such as depression, anxiety, low self-esteem, learning disabilities, or possibly drug or alcohol abuse.

The key to determining the seriousness of the

problem is one of degree and balance. While conflict and power struggles are a necessary part of your daughter's separating from you and becoming her own person, constant and ongoing rule breaking are another story. There should be a balance between cooperation/connection and conflict/confrontation. If your days are filled with conflict and confrontation, seek professional help. Sometimes a third party who is impartial can help negotiate an agreement that your daughter is willing to abide by. Or if the source of these ongoing conflicts is deeper, your daughter will get the help that she needs.

Hot Tips

☞ How do you know if your daughter is in trouble or just being a teenager? Is she eating a lot more or a lot less? Is there a significant change in her sleeping habits? Has her school performance changed? Is she withdrawn, or more irritable and edgy than usual? If your answer is "yes" to more than one of these questions, get help. While there may not be a serious problem, don't take any chances.

☞ Stay connected with other parents, especially the parents of your daughter's friends. Knowing that you are in contact with her friends' parents will reduce the number of times your daughter can successfully "pull the wool over your eyes." It can help you and your daughter if you get together with her friends' parents and you can all agree on some rules, such as curfews and places your daughters can go. It will be much easier for her to accept limits if her friends have the same ones.

☞ Stay tuned in to what is happening with teens in your community. Go to parenting classes, attend drug information sessions, and participate in a support network of drug- and alcohol-free parties. Let your daughter know, by your behavior and your investment of your time and energy, that these are serious issues that you care about.

☞ Peer pressure is one of the "givens" for all teens. So, it is very likely that your daughter is going to feel some pressure to experiment with drugs, alcohol, sex, or shoplifting sometime during her teen years. What can you do? Give your daughter accurate information about what the effects of these behaviors can be on her future. Don't use scare tactics and don't exaggerate the truth. Provide her with concrete case examples of how "good" kids have really messed up their lives by making some very bad choices that have had long-term consequences. Make it safe for your daughter to talk to you. If she thinks you will only yell and restrict her for "stepping over the line," she won't confide in you at all.

☞ If you constantly focus on your own or your daughter's looks, she is more likely to have trouble accepting her own body. While complimenting your daughter when she looks nice is important, it is critical to support and encourage her strengths and talents beyond just her looks. Be sure to praise your daughter for her accomplishments and relationships with others; they are far more important than her looks.

☞ Eating disorders are not only very serious but can also be deadly. If your daughter seems overly obsessed with her looks, if she seems to be watching everything she eats all of the time, if she is constantly exercising to lose weight, get help right away. Don't try to handle it yourself; eating disorders require professional help.

☞ It is your responsibility as a parent to ensure that your daughter has accurate information about sex. If you feel hesitant or embarrassed, get over it! But, if you find that no matter how hard you try, you're still so uncomfortable that you just can't open your mouth, find someone else—a relative, her physician, a youth group leader—to help. No matter what, be sure your daughter is informed and has someone to turn to when she needs information or just needs to talk.

☞ Your daughter's emerging sexuality can be a struggle and sometimes a source of great internal conflict. This is especially true if her sexual orientation does not develop along "standard" lines. Girls who are lesbians or bisexual need their parents' acceptance, love, and support. While your daughter's sexual orientation might be hard for you to deal with, she needs you! A parent support group can help you a lot.

☞ The ways in which you and other members of your family express anger provide the model for your daughter. Through your own behavior, you can demonstrate how to express anger in appropriate ways. Let your daughter "listen in" when you are telling someone how angry you are so she can learn from your example. You need to allow your daughter to vent her anger as well.

☞ Women have just as much of a right to express their anger as men do. Teach your daughter the difference between being assertive and being aggressive. Being assertive means that you can express your own feelings, including anger, without dismissing or trampling over the needs and feelings of others. Help your daughter be assertive and let her know that aggression is just as unacceptable in men as it is in women.

☞ Whether you like it or not, you cannot control when your daughter chooses to have sex. What you *can* do is give her the tools and resources to make a wise and healthy decision for herself. Let her know that a decision to have sex is an important one and can have serious consequences and risks to her physical and mental health. In the end, you must accept the fact that the decision is hers.

☞ While feeling sad or down is normal, it is important for you to know the difference between when your daughter is going through a tough time and and when she is depressed. Difficulty concentrating, headaches, stomachaches, loss of interest in things she used to enjoy, irritability, withdrawal, sadness, and isolation are all signs of depression. Depression can be treated. Talk with your daughter's doctor.

☞ Your daughter needs to know how to keep herself safe and protect herself from physical danger, including date rape. Make sure your daughter is aware of how using drugs and alcohol can lead to date rape. Ask your daughter to consider taking a self-defense class.

☞ Know what is going on in your daughter's life. Take the time to meet her friends, follow her schoolwork and activities, and know where she is. Believe it or not, these are the most effective things you can do to keep your daughter physically and emotionally safe.

☞ At times, your daughter will struggle with normal feelings of anxiety and depression. You can help her develop the coping skills to manage difficult times. For example: teach your daughter how helpful it can be to talk with you or a friend; help your daughter learn to identify problems early on and not ignore them; teach her problem-solving skills and praise her success when she solves a difficult problem. Boost your daughter's self-esteem by reminding her of other difficult times she has successfully made it through, and help her to identify the coping skills she has successfully used in the past.

☞ All families go through difficult times. Whether it is a death, a divorce, a move, or money problems, it is more than likely that your daughter will experience some trauma growing up. You can help your daughter by encouraging her to talk about her feelings, giving her accurate and honest information, and letting her know about specific resources outside of the immediate family that she can turn to.

☞ Most adolescents will test some of the rules by arguing, "forgetting" them, or simply ignoring them or breaking them. This is normal. If you have worked on compromising and negotiating, and your daughter continues to ignore or break reasonable rules, it might mean that she has bigger problems that call for professional help.

4

How Can I Help Her Feel Good About Herself? Building Strength and Resiliency in Adolescent Girls

I'm very lucky. My daughters, Lilly and Deana, and I get along pretty well, and I think they both still look up to me and see me as a role model. I know how important it is for me to continue to be a part of their lives. But, sometimes I wonder if I'm being too intrusive. I'm just not sure where to draw the line: When should I try to help them, and when should I step back?

I want to be a good parent, and I know that a big part of my "job" is to help my daughters develop positive self-esteem and confidence. I want them to feel good about themselves and be able to balance all the demands and pressures they will be confronted with. As they get older, I want my daughters to become more and more independent—to be able to take risks but to also use good judgment in deciding what risks to take. I want my daughters to treat their friends with care and respect and to see themselves as equal to and as capable as their male peers.

I want all of these things for Lilly and Deana —but I'm not sure how to make it all happen. I talk with them a lot, but I can't believe talking is enough. I try to be a good role model, but of course I make mistakes—I'm certainly not perfect. I wonder if there's something else I should be saying or doing? Am I doing enough? Am I doing the right things?—*Kim Lee, mother of Lilly and Deana, ages 13 and 17*

How can I help my daughter develop and maintain positive self-esteem? *Sue T.*

How your daughter feels about herself, her "self-esteem," starts to develop well before the teen years. Your task now is to do all you can to enhance her positive feelings about herself. The best way to accomplish this is to encourage and support her in identifying and exploring her gifts, interests, and abilities. Help your daughter to look at this time of her life as a "buffet," which offers her the chance to examine and experiment with all kinds of ideas and interests.

Encourage your daughter to explore different activities, to take on new challenges, and to find those things that bring her pleasure.

While it is important that you emphasize to your daughter that she learn to stick with things and not give up too easily, this needs to be balanced with an understanding that adolescence is also a time for your daughter to try new things and explore new ideas. Don't insist that your daughter stick with an activity if she feels like she is no longer interested in it or would rather use the time to explore another interest. Deciding to stop one activity and do something else does not necessarily make your daughter a "quitter." It might simply mean that she wants to taste something different from the buffet. However, if an activity or interest requires a financial commitment (such as private music or art lessons) or is one in which others are counting on her (such as a team sport), it is fair to ask your daughter to agree on a minimum commitment in advance.

While your daughter can probably use some guidance about how she might go about exploring her interests and abilities, true self-esteem comes from the feeling that she, herself, can make good things happen in her life. This means that your daughter will have to take some risks. And you will have to tolerate some anxiety when she does.

Remember, it is OK for your daughter to fail; your job is to help and encourage her to pick herself up when she falls. These experiences are an important part of your daughter's adolescence.

* * *

Some girls enter their teen years with shaky self-esteem. Although they may seem well put together on the outside, on the inside many teens don't have the strength or resilience they need to weather the possibly stormy teen years.

Why do some girls start off on shaky ground? There is really no simple answer. Family problems or conflicts, poor role models, learning disabilities, genetic vulnerability, or physical disabilities can all make it difficult for an adolescent girl to develop positive self-esteem. However, remember that during adolescence, one day your daughter may seem on top of the world, and on another day she may be in the pits. This is normal and not necessarily a sign of low self-esteem. The time to be concerned is when and if your daughter seems to be on a general downward spiral and when she doesn't bounce back from failures or disappointments.

For girls with shaky self-esteem, something more than a supportive atmosphere is needed. They need strong guidance and help to find their strengths and talents. They need extra encouragement to try new things. They need you to directly and clearly tell them that they have done a good job, are making progress, or should simply be more patient.

If your support and encouragement alone are not enough, talk to professionals who can help you. For example, if your daughter is having trouble in school, and in spite of her efforts can't seem to be successful, an evaluation of her academic abilities and learning style may be in order. Talk with your daughter's teachers, school psychologist, guidance counselor, or pediatrician about where you can get help. In many states, school districts provide evaluations free of charge. You won't know what resources are out there until you start investigating.

Some of the best resources are the parents of other teens. Believe it or not, they are also struggling with many of the same or similar issues. Connecting with other parents can often provide you with new information and with emotional support as well.

How can dads acknowledge their daughter's physical beauty without reinforcing the emphasis that culture places on beauty? *Jackson S.*

There is no doubt that in our culture, physical beauty is highly valued. Even if you disagree with the overemphasis our culture places on beauty, you cannot ignore the fact that, at this time in your daughter's life, physical appearance is extremely important to her. One of a father's tasks is to affirm this aspect of his daughter's self-esteem without giving her the message that beauty is everything, or even close to the top of the list.

Dads, in particular, serve as a very powerful influence on their daughters with regard to how much their daughters rely on appearance for their self-esteem. If your daughter sees her father as "too taken" or drawn to women's beauty, to the exclusion of other attributes, she will get the message that her appearance is the most important part of her, especially when it comes to men. Dads need to be careful to comment on the attractiveness of *all* aspects of a woman, not just her physical beauty. And the same holds true when commenting on the attractiveness of their own daughters.

There are almost endless ways in which fathers can compliment their daughters about attributes other than their physical appearance. What about her emotional strengths, such as warmth, sense of humor, loyalty, courage, and empathy? And how about her intellectual strengths and academic successes? And what about her commonsense and problem-solving skills? By asking themselves these questions, fathers can help to make sure that their daughters get the message that "beauty" includes the inside as well as the outside.

So what exactly can a dad say to his daughter about her looks? It can be as simple as stating the obvious:

- "You're developing into a lovely young woman."
- "Did you know that you have very pretty eyes?"
- "Your skin is beautiful."
- "You look like you're in really good shape from the exercise you're doing."

It is equally important to let your daughter know, in a gentle way, if she is overdoing some aspect of her experimentation with new forms of dress and makeup. Honest feedback, delivered with sensitivity, will allow your daughter to "trust" your positive feedback. For example, you might say something like, "You look great, but I think you may have overdone the lipstick." Or, "I don't like thinking about the comments guys might make when they see you dressed like that." Your daughter is most likely to consider such feedback if you have a history of giving her lots of compliments and not just about her appearance. If the only time you comment on your daughter's appearance is when you have a criticism to make, she'll probably blow you off without giving much thought to your feedback.

Fathers have the ability to help make their daughters feel like beautiful women, inside and out. But in order to accomplish this, fathers need to be thoughtful and careful about the comments they make.

* * *

Men are subject to the same cultural messages that overemphasize feminine beauty as are their daughters. As a father, it is important to stay aware of these messages and how they influence your own thoughts and behavior. Fathers can help to counteract the stereotypes and overemphasis that our culture places on female beauty by reminding their daughters that ideal images are unrealistic and the emphasis on beauty is just too much. For example, when you are relaxing on a Sunday night and watching TV together, take the opportunity to comment to your daughter that some of the women in the media who she may think are beautiful actually have dangerous eating disorders, like anorexia and bulimia. And if a "blonde bimbo" appears on the screen, let your daughter know that you don't find her the least bit attractive since her lack of brains detracts from her overall beauty.

Ask your daughter to think about how she feels about the models in fashion or teen magazines. Talk with her about how these models portray unrealistic images of female beauty and how these women are either starving themselves or are airbrushed to look perfect.

Fathers who pay attention to how our culture has conditioned them to overemphasize female beauty can do a better job in communicating a balanced message to their daughters, one in which beauty includes both the inside and the outside.

How can adults positively influence adolescent girls without being overbearing? *Mary D.*

There are three important words to keep in mind if you want to positively influence your adolescent daughter: listen, respect, and encourage.

1. Listen: Listening is the best way to find out what your daughter is thinking and feeling. Careful listening will enable you to comment about things that matter to her. Ask your daughter what she thinks about anything that might be a part of her life. For example, ask her about the music she listens to. What draws her to it? The verse, the beat, the singer? Ask her what she thinks about some of the rules in her school. Are they fair? Unfair? How would she change them if she could? The more your daughter feels you are interested in how *she* thinks and feels about *her* life, the more she will share with you and the more she will respect and consider your opinion. But remember, in this process, you need to be sure to listen to and understand her point of view before you add your own.

2. Respect: Respect is something that must be earned, by parents as well as teens. The old-fashioned idea that children should respect and obey their parents *just* because they are parents is long gone. While you might wish this wasn't the case, think about why this change has happened: You have asked your daughter *not* to follow authority blindly; you have encouraged her to be assertive; you have taught her to evaluate what adults and her peers tell her before she makes a decision. You have encouraged her to think for herself and, at times, to question "the rules." So,

it is only natural that she is going to question your authority as well. Just because she questions you doesn't mean she doesn't respect you.

Respect develops and thrives when you communicate that the other person has a right to his or her own thoughts, ideas, and feelings. For example, while you may not agree with your daughter's decision to drop out of an extracurricular activity, such as band or chorus, you need to respect her right to make some of her own decisions. You need to be careful not to give your daughter the message that you don't respect her simply because you don't agree with her. Your daughter will make some self-defeating decisions along the way. She's supposed to! It's part of her learning process. If you want to positively influence your daughter, you must respect her as a person. And in return, your daughter will eventually come to respect you for who you are, not necessarily because you're in charge and still have power over her.

3. Encourage: Finally, encourage your daughter to be true to herself. While the kid you see in front of you might seem like a totally different person on the surface, her basic qualities are already in place. Encourage your daughter to be true to those enduring qualities that help define who she is. Encourage honesty, responsibility, loyalty, and any other values that help define her integrity. Let her know that even while you may have fierce dis-

agreements, you never question her basic qualities as a person.

* * *

The best way to avoid being overbearing is to remember to listen first and talk second. Your daughter will experience you as controlling and rigid if it seems like you just want things done your way and don't listen to her opinion or perspective. The best way to avoid giving your daughter this feeling is to avoid starting a conversation by saying what *you* want or what you need. There will be plenty of time for you to speak.

First, find out what your daughter wants or needs. You don't have to agree, but you do have to listen long enough to hear her out. Then, try repeating back to her a summary of what you think she has said, and ask her if you got it right. This will really make your daughter feel like you have listened to her. After this, your comments will be a lot easier for her to hear.

Teens often think that if you do not agree with them, it is because you haven't heard them. So, if you really work to let your daughter know that you have tried hard to listen to her, she is much more likely to really hear what you have to say. She may not agree with you, but she is more likely to respect your right to have a different opinion.

How can we help highly driven girls balance the demands of school, sports, and other activities with finding the time for the comfort and support of family and friends? *Dylan F.*

As you probably know, there are some people who just never learn to balance their priorities. It is important to remember that this is not a skill that any of us were born with. In a very practical sense, your daughter may need help in learning how to weigh and set her own priorities. While you can assist her with the process, you must remember that her priorities may not be the same as the ones you would set for her, and unless things are really out of whack, you need to respect her choices. And, if your daughter feels respected, she will probably be much more open to your suggestions.

You might suggest that your daughter make a list of all the activities and responsibilities she has. If her list seems incomplete, you can offer to add anything you think she has left out. Then suggest that she divide her list into two different parts: the "have to" list and the "want to" list. This will help her sort out what is truly important to her, what is optional, and what she can let go of. Don't be surprised if the words *relaxation, do nothing,* or *down time* don't appear on her lists at all. Many teens forget how essential it is to have some time that is totally their own, with nothing they need to do. Parents also forget that down time is not optional: It is essential. Other essential items are time for family and friends. So be sure that these are on her have-to list as well. Then, suggest that she arrange the items on the lists so that they are ranked in order of importance. The most important ones go on top, and the least important ones go on the bottom. This concrete activity can help your daughter get a clearer picture of the priorities in her life and help her decide what she wants to keep and what she wants to let go of.

Your daughter will very quickly learn that life doesn't necessarily proceed according to our expectations, and at times priorities just have to be shifted. Her lists will probably need to be modified and changed on a regular basis. Learning how to set priorities will not only help her now but in the years to come.

* * *

Today, more than ever, teens are under pressure to achieve in school, on the playing field, through volunteer work, as well as in numerous other activities. Because there are so many outside sources of pressure, like standardized tests, Advanced Placement courses, coaches for whom winning is all that counts —your daughter may need you to provide a release from the pressure, not add to it. As her parent, you must make sure that you don't drive your daughter too hard. While motivating and encouraging your daughter is important, be careful that you don't make her so anxious that she can't find time to relax and comfortably connect with her family and friends.

Learning to balance the demands of life with her own needs for comfort and support is one of your daughter's greatest challenges. As with many things, she will not learn to give time to herself, her family, or her friends if you don't. After all, what she sees at home is going to have a great impact on her. If you do a pretty good job of balancing your own life, your daughter will learn from you. Do you make time for your friends? Are there definite family times that are protected in your busy schedule? Are you flexible enough to shift priorities as demands change? Teens are very sensitive to hypocrisy and double messages. They learn and imitate what we do, not what we say or preach.

Remember, you've had many years to develop your "balancing act." Your daughter will need time to figure this out for herself. In addition, the demands on your daughter not only keep changing but also are steadily increasing, so she has to learn how to continually make adjustments. So take a close, honest look at your own life. Do you stop from time to time to reevaluate the balance in your own life? How you model the balancing act of work, household and personal responsibilities, play, relaxation, and social time will have a significant impact on how your daughter balances these things in her own life.

* * *

Give your daughter plenty of notice about family gatherings or events, and don't assume that just because it is the very highest priority to you that it will be for your daughter as well. Remember, during the teen years, it is normal for friends to take more of your daughter's time than her family does. And, it may seem like they are more important than her family. In spite of how it seems, however, underneath it all, family is still important to her, so you should make sure that your daughter invests at least some of her time with her family. It is this time that will provide the foundation for her long-term connections and relationships with her own children.

It might help if, at the beginning of the school year, you talk with your daughter about her schedule and the need to have balance in her life. Suggest that she carve out and protect some time for herself, her family, and her friends. Don't be afraid to place some restrictions on her to help her have "time off." For example, it is OK to say that an activity every day after school is too much. It is important to remember that your daughter may not thank you now for making her slow down. She may be so caught up in achieving and participating in activities that she finds your restrictions annoying. But, it is OK to be firm about it.

How can my daughter's teachers encourage her to be independent and take risks?
Hillary W.

Since teachers are important role models for adolescent girls, they can do a great deal to foster teens' independence and exploration of the world by encouraging them to speak out in class, by supporting them in developing their own ideas in the subject matter, and by encouraging and supporting them in developing their own academic interests and specialties. Teachers play an important role in helping adolescent girls find and keep their "voices." By asking girls to talk from their experiences, beliefs, feelings, and thoughts, teachers can encourage them to think for themselves, to evaluate how far they can stretch in new and unknown situations and circumstances, and to voice their own ideas and opinions.

Teachers can make sure that their students are exposed to material about women who have become successful and independent through their willingness to take healthy risks. They can encourage girls to respond intellectually to their male peers in the classroom. Teachers are also in a powerful position to comment about trends and aspects of the adolescent subculture. They can lead discussions about the positive and negative aspects of the subculture in which your adolescent daughter lives.

Whenever possible, support your daughter's teachers by letting them know how much you value their work. But be aware that as your daughter gets older, she is more likely to resent or be embarrassed by your direct involvement with her teachers. However, you can still be involved in curriculum committees, parent–teacher associations, career days, and other school events.

* * *

In most cases, your daughter's teachers are committed to creating an environment of intellectual and emotional growth and independence. One of the most important things that teachers can do to encourage adolescent girls' independence is to make sure that there is gender equality in their classrooms. Teachers can help to ensure this equality by

- making sure that girls and boys are called on with equal frequency and encouraged equally to respond to questions and to present material
- assigning girls to head group projects and present group results
- offering girls opportunities to take on leadership positions on an equal basis with boys
- making sure that in their classrooms they are as positive and encouraging to girls as to boys, appropriately praising members of both genders
- directly addressing any behavior that discriminates against students because of their gender
- making it clear to their students that their work will be judged on its merits, not on their gender.

As a parent, be sure to communicate your support

and appreciation for teachers' efforts to ensure gender equality in their classrooms because of its importance in encouraging your daughter to be independent and to take healthy risks. And be sure to speak up about any concerns you may have.

What are the positive ways in which adolescent girls can respond to the stresses of today's society? *Norma N.*

Learning coping skills to deal with the stresses of today's society is very important not only for your daughter's life right now but also for her ability to manage the inevitable crises that will cross her path in the future. Adolescent girls today are growing up in a world that is hectic and fast-paced, a world that is not always happy, safe, or secure. TV and newspaper headlines highlight tragedies. Although most have taken place far away, the impact of some events, such as school shootings, hits especially close to home. Your daughter may have already encountered a personal, up-close tragedy, like an assault, rape, death, or suicide of someone she knows.

One of the most positive ways you can help your daughter respond to the stresses in her world is to encourage her to become involved in activities that are designed not only for her own personal growth but also for the betterment of society. Help her to learn about the joy and satisfaction that come from giving. It is important that your daughter feels empowered to make changes in the world around her, in any small ways that she can.

Your daughter can volunteer time at a soup kitchen or help distribute meals to the homeless; she can make donations to a charity; she can distribute flyers in her school to make other teens aware of an issue that is important to her, like students against drunk driving; or she can serve as a Big Sister to an underprivileged young child. The list of possibilities is endless—the point is to help your daughter to not be a passive victim of society's pressures but rather to be an active participant in finding solutions.

Adolescent girls often display significant amounts of empathy, compassion, and caring. They have found vehicles to express these qualities through organizations that deal with issues like drunk driving, AIDS and other diseases, homelessness, animal rights and welfare, and many more. Many adolescent girls also reach out to help friends in need, whether it be with homework, listening to personal problems, or encouraging them to try new activities. Adolescent girls develop and maintain networks of friendships in which they can talk about every imaginable subject and feeling. It is these activities and networks of friendships that provide them with the feelings of connection and accomplishment that are critical in dealing with the stresses of living in our world today.

* * *

Getting adolescent girls involved in positive, stress-reducing activities early in their teen years is one of the best ways to help them deal with the pressures they will experience throughout their lives. Try to encourage your daughter to participate in at least one nonstressful activity that brings her feelings of pleasure and satisfaction each day. Ask her to take a few minutes to think about what activities help her to relax. Is it listening to music? Watching TV? Talking on the phone to friends? Taking a catnap? Curling up with a good book? Some teens find relaxation through a hobby, playing an instrument, or working on an art project. Some like to write in their journal or diary. Or is physical activity more relaxing to her, like exercising, running, or dancing? Whatever it is, encourage your daughter to make time for the activities that help her feel less pressured and stressed.

You might also encourage your daughter to explore new avenues of stress reduction. Maybe the two of you can enroll in a yoga or meditation class together. Remember that physical activity has been proven to be one of the best stress reducers, not just for teens but for adults too. So you might try jogging together, or taking a dance class, or even just going for a long walk with her.

Tell your daughter about the things that you do to deal with the stress in your life, like taking a hot bath, gardening, watching a football game, or going to the gym to work out. Many teens know very little about how their parents actually cope. You want your daughter to know that taking the time to physically and mentally relax helps us all to cope with the inevitable pressures of today's society.

How can fathers be better influences? How can they more positively impact their daughters' lives? *John J.*

There are multitudes of ways in which fathers can positively influence their daughters. And most of them begin with actually spending time together. The more time a father spends with his daughter, the more positive the result. And, in direct contrast, the more a daughter feels unimportant, ignored, or even rejected by her father, the more vulnerable she is to developing low self-esteem in regard to men. In addition, she will also be more likely to engage in negative risk-taking behavior to get male attention. Far too many fathers (and in some cases even mothers) believe that their teenage daughters do not really need very much of their fathers' attention and involvement in their lives. *This is just not true.*

Adolescent girls both want and need their fathers. Fathers are almost always the "first man" in their life. Their attention, support, and positive feedback provide their daughters with something that mothers and other female role models cannot: *male* attention and affirmation. Let's face it: For most adolescent girls, the same compliment when it comes from Mom is different than when it comes from Dad.

And, if a girl's father is not available, for whatever reason, it is important to try to help her find and connect with another adult male—possibly a grandfather or an uncle who is interested in her life and wants to spend time with her.

Many fathers are much more involved with their daughters when they are "little girls," and they do not even notice the growing disconnection with their daughters as they develop into teenagers and young women. If you ask these fathers what happened, many of them say they didn't even realize that so much distance had come between them! There are also many fathers who want to stay connected and involved with their daughters as they get older but simply do not know how. Some fathers believe that because of their daughter's emerging sexuality, they are "supposed" to move away so as to be sure not to do or say anything inappropriate. Others report that they feel "pushed away"; that their daughters now seem to reject their attempts to do things together. Still others feel that their wives are giving them the message that they are no longer needed or that they are "inadequate" in knowing how to relate to their adolescent daughters. And all too often, they are right—their wives *are* giving them this message! And finally, at the same time that their daughters are moving into adolescence, many fathers are at the height of their careers and earning power and are torn between being the "good providers" they have been taught to be and finding more time for their families. In the end, far too many fathers find themselves more and more involved with their work and less and less involved with their daughters. Some of these fathers eventually realize that they have become strangers to their daughters and often have no idea how it happened.

While joint projects and hobbies, or shared interests or activities, are easy ways to stay connected, even the simple exchange of information about each other's day will make your daughter feel important. If the logistics of meetings or activities make it difficult to have face-to-face contact, a quick phone call, or sending an e-mail to touch base, will go a long way to nurture and maintain the feeling of connection. A note left on the kitchen table before a big exam or tryouts for a sport or the school play makes a huge difference in how much a daughter feels acknowledged by her father. And, whenever possible, fathers should include their daughters in work, hobbies, and chores around the house.

* * *

You can't expect to have any influence on your daughter if you don't spend time with her. Setting aside a special time each week, or at least every other week, to do something with your daughter—even if it's just having breakfast or lunch together—can mean a great deal to her. If you encounter resistance —like your daughter telling you she doesn't have time, or she thinks it's weird—try a slightly different approach. One father took some time after picking up his daughter from her violin lesson each Saturday to stop at her favorite music store on the way home.

This became their special time. Years later, his daughter told him how much those times meant to her.

Try to attend as many of your daughter's activities, such as plays, sports events, and concerts, as possible. While many fathers find it difficult to attend after-school events, even making it to one or two can mean a tremendous amount to your daughter. It gives her a very special feeling of self-worth and value when you have taken the time from work to come and watch her perform, particularly in front of her peers and teachers.

For many fathers, it takes a conscious commitment and "insistence" to find the ways to stay connected with their adolescent daughters. Fathers who know and understand how important they are for their daughter's growth and development seem to have an easier time sticking with the often bumpy road that comes with being the father of a teenage girl.

* * *

Fathers are the role models for the kinds of men their daughters often choose. Therefore, how you as a father treat your daughter can set the framework for how she will expect to be treated by other men. Most important is *respect*. Fathers should show respect for women by avoiding sexist jokes and other ways of putting women down. If someone makes a sexist joke or acts in a sexist manner, a father can express his disapproval by saying something to point out the prejudice. Girls are more likely to have positive and healthy relationships with men when their fathers have shown respect for women, treated them with equality, and have made an effort to communicate openly and honestly with them.

Teenagers learn by example, so fathers need to be careful to practice what they preach. If they model "male chauvinism," they will teach their daughters that they are second-class citizens because they are female. This does not mean that chivalry should be dead. Opening a door, offering to carry a heavy suitcase, or other thoughtful behaviors are not chauvinistic—they are simply caring, thoughtful, and respectful. A "feminist" father can open a door for his daughter and still raise an independent, self-reliant woman.

As her father, you should make a special point to communicate to your daughter the ways in which you see her strengths, not only the ways you fear for her safety or see her fragility. And remember, dads who can talk about topics such as sexuality, relationships, feelings, vulnerabilities, and even about how men and boys feel about women and girls make themselves available to their daughters in important ways.

How can adolescent girls be encouraged to regard themselves as equal to adolescent boys? *Daria C.*

Unfortunately, in spite of the many strides we have made toward equality, even today women are not always regarded or treated as equal to men. There is still a long way to go. Therefore, it is important to talk with your daughter about the historical and cultural ways that girls and women have been oppressed and treated as second-class citizens. Tell her how even now, women in some parts of the world have made very little progress toward equal status with men. As a parent, you can help to provide a perspective on how pervasive these attitudes have been and how only by challenging the dominant male culture have women been able to move toward greater equality.

It is important to make sure your daughter sees herself as equal to her male peers. One of the best ways to do this is to be a good role model. Demonstrate equality, respect, and autonomy in your relationships with the opposite sex. Ensure that household responsibilities are not gender-typed: Boys can do laundry and scrub toilets; girls can mow lawns and take out trash.

Encourage your daughter to consider hobbies or activities that might still be seen as primarily for guys. Support her experimentation and participation in a full spectrum of activities—from wrestling to knitting, from basketball to cheerleading, from auto repair to cooking. Encourage your daughter to have male friends. Support her involvement in activities in which she will learn to become comfortable with her male peers. This is the time in her life when she needs to build her confidence as a woman in "men's activities" as well as her confidence as a woman with men.

Whenever and wherever you can, help your daughter to support the equality of women and challenge those who treat women as second-class citizens.

* * *

Parents, teachers, and other adults need to emphasize the fact that while women, including adolescent girls, are not always treated equally, they *are already* equal to men. A woman's competence, intelligence, and potential are not limited by her gender. Her inner worth is no different. This does not necessarily mean that girls are always identical to boys in their abilities but that they are equally valued; what girls offer is no less important than what boys offer. The skills that a girl has are just as valuable as the skills that a boy has, even when they are different. For example, in sports, a boy may exhibit more physical strength and power, but a girl may be more flexible and agile. Both attributes are valuable and important in most sports, such as gymnastics, hockey, and tennis. One is not less important than the other. Thus, although women and men are equal in worth, they are not identical. And, most important, the potential for both genders to expand their skills is almost limitless!

How can you best encourage your daughter to feel equal to her male peers? Certainly, telling her that she is as good as a boy is important. But what is far more important is that the adults in your daughter's life *demonstrate* equality by accepting and treating girls and boys, and men and women, as equals.

How can we get adolescent girls to care for and watch out for each other?
Abigail R.

It is difficult and sometimes painful to observe adolescent girls being insensitive or oblivious to the needs and well-being of others, including their female friends. Have you ever observed your daughter cancel plans with one of her friends when something "better" comes along? Have you ever seen her drop a girlfriend like a hot potato when a new boyfriend comes on the scene? Or, have you ever noticed how your daughter and a couple of her friends will get together and tear down one of their previous "friends," or even bad-mouth or "dis" a friend who is just not with them at that moment? While this kind of behavior is not at all unusual, this does not mean that it should be ignored or simply accepted as a passing phase.

If you see or hear your daughter being insensitive, find a time when you can talk with her about how important it is for her and her friends to take care of and watch out for each other. Ask her to think about how she would feel if she were being ignored, dumped, or treated as if she were no longer cared about or important. Ask her how she thinks it would feel if the other girls didn't look out for her. (And don't forget that asking a question is almost always more helpful than telling your daughter what she should do, and it's certainly better than criticizing or judging her.) The goal here is for you to raise her consciousness, not lecture or judge her.

Your daughter may seem insensitive or uncaring because she often does not stop long enough to really think about how her behavior will affect someone else. By asking questions that help your daughter to think and reflect, you will be helping her to become a good friend and you will be teaching her the importance of watching out for her friends. Learning to pay attention to the needs and feelings of others takes time, so don't expect a single conversation or experience to do the trick.

* * *

Being a member of a team is one of the best vehicles for teaching girls to care for and watch out for each other. Through their participation in team sports, girls learn the importance of "us" rather than just "me." Historically, girls were relegated to the sidelines where they could cheer for boys. But girls now have many more opportunities to play and excel in a variety of team sports. They can now play recreational or competitive sports, including basketball, softball, soccer, and volleyball, to name a few. Research has shown that girls who play team sports are more likely to develop a philosophy that cooperation with teammates works toward success for all. Team coaches often remind players, "There is no 'i' in team."

If your daughter is not interested in sports, you might encourage her to become involved in other activities in which she is part of a team. There are volunteer groups, such as Habitat for Humanity, which sponsors women-only projects, in which women work together toward a common goal. Through teamwork, your daughter can learn to care about and watch out for others, not just herself.

Hot Tips

☞ You can support the development of your daughter's positive self-esteem by helping her to identify her talents and encouraging her to explore her interests. Let her know that her teen years are a time for healthy experimentation. While you don't want her to be a quitter, it is important for her to try different things.

☞ Fathers play a very important role in helping their daughters to value their intelligence, talents, and personality as much, if not more, than their physical attributes. Try to ensure that the male attention your daughter receives is focused on who she is on the inside, not just on how she looks on the outside.

☞ Listen, respect, and encourage: These are the best ways to create the kind of relationship that will allow you to have some influence on your daughter. While dictating, demanding, and judging might change her behavior at the moment, their effects will be short-lived.

☞ If you want your daughter to really hear your opinion or perspective, listen first and talk second. Find out what your daughter wants or thinks before you tell her what you want or think. Try summarizing what she has said to let her know that you have really heard her. Listening and understanding don't mean you are agreeing, and it might make her more receptive to hearing your views and opinions.

☞ Learning how to manage time and how to set priorities takes time and practice. Don't expect your daughter to suddenly figure it all out. She's supposed to "mess up." That's how we all learn.

☞ Learning how to balance our responsibilities with our "wants" and "wishes" can be tough for any of us. Try helping your daughter make a list of her "have tos" and her "wants," and then consider ways she can balance them. Let her know that you want her to have fun and enjoy life, as well as meet her responsibilities.

☞ If *you* seek perfection, your daughter will think *she* should also. Acknowledge your mistakes, talk about them, and when it is appropriate, apologize. Remind your daughter that no one is perfect!

☞ While it is most often unintentional, many schools and teachers still treat girls differently from boys. It is up to you, as her parent, to pay close attention to the messages your daughter gets from her school and her teachers. Ask your daughter if she gets called on as much as the boys, if girls are encouraged to take math and science classes, and if they have access to the same team sports. Consider meeting with her teachers or the school administration to address any inequalities she is experiencing in school.

☞ Parents and teachers of adolescent girls who treat them as equal to boys, and who teach them to speak up and not accept unequal treatment, make it possible for these girls to both see themselves as equal and help them to insist on equal treatment. If you see that your daughter is not receiving equal treatment, encourage and support her in speaking out on her own behalf. Don't ever suggest that she is deserving of less than or should accept anything but total equality.

☞ Adolescence is often stressful. Help your daughter identify her own list of stress-reducing activities, such as listening to music, working out, or reading a book. Encourage her to engage in at least one stress-reducing activity a day. And, try doing the same for yourself!

☞ It is a myth that adolescent girls need their mothers but not their fathers (or good father figures). Unfortunately, although there have been some changes, mothers still play the dominant role in the lives of most adolescent girls. Fathers need to do more and be more involved. They need to make sure, and if necessary *insist*, that they be given the opportunity to parent their daughters.

☞ Teach your daughter to watch out for, support, and help her friends. Encourage her to reach out to an adult if she thinks a friend is in serious trouble.

5

How Will She Ever Become an Independent Woman? Helping Adolescent Girls Prepare for the Future

My daughter Yvette is becoming a woman, an adult. She'll be on her own pretty soon, and she'll be making more and more of her own decisions. To me, it feels like the future is right around the corner. Time rushes by so quickly. I need to prepare Yvette for what lies ahead. I know that now is the time for her to start thinking more about her future. I try to impress this on her, but most of the time she seems to be focused only on today. Whenever I try to talk with her about college or career choices, she says, "not now" or "I'll talk to you later" or "I know already, my guidance counselor told us everything." She's always telling me how I worry too much.

I want to encourage Yvette so she will head in the right direction. I want her to maximize her potential and her capabilities. I want her to strive to do well academically, to be self-sufficient, and to learn how to spend her money wisely. But I'm not sure about the best way to influence her. Should I tell her about my own experiences as a teenager? Should I insist that she listen to me? What if I'm being too optimistic about the possibilities in front of her? Am I raising her hopes too high? As a woman, will there really be more choices for her than there were for her mother? And how can I help prepare her for the future when everything around us is changing so much and so quickly? I don't know what the future holds for her.

I had it really rough when I was a kid. I want it to be different for my daughter. If I can, I want to smooth the way for her. How can I best help her?—*Leroy, father of Yvette, age 18*

What steps can I take to encourage my daughter to choose a math or science career? *Cory O.*

It is fascinating to see how your daughter's curiosity and interests begin to combine with her skills and talents. As this happens, it is normal for you to begin to think about or imagine the kind of career your daughter would enjoy and succeed in. It is natural and normal for parents to have hopes and dreams for their children. The trick is to be careful not to impose *your* hopes and dreams on her.

So, while you might *want* your daughter to choose a career in math or science, the choice *must* be hers … not yours. You cannot and should not *push* your daughter into any career. However, as her parent, you do play an important role in determining the range of options that your daughter might consider.

If you believe that your daughter has some talent and interest in the sciences or math, encourage her to take more than the required math and science classes and to consider careers in these fields. Encourage your daughter to look for after-school activities that will help her explore these interests. Often, hospitals and research centers have visiting days or special programs for teenagers interested in careers in the sciences. Watch for career exploration days in your community, and encourage your daughter to talk with as many people as she can about how they came to their particular career choice.

With this approach, your daughter will feel your support and encouragement to consider many different career choices and to take classes that will help her to further explore her interests. In the end, your daughter will be happiest with her career choice if she is able to achieve a reasonable degree of success and enjoy what she is doing. Don't try to push your daughter into a field that does not draw from her skills and talents or that does not seem to interest her. Your daughter needs your ongoing encouragement and support in helping her explore *her own* talents and strengths, not in becoming what you think she should be. You should not try to control her choices.

* * *

If your daughter seems to have an interest in math or science, support her by giving her books and articles about women in science and math. It can be an inspiration for her to learn about famous women scientists and mathematicians. It is also important to help your daughter meet and interact with women in her own community who are in the math and science fields.

Unfortunately, many adolescent girls still believe that they are less likely than boys to succeed in the academic work required to prepare for a career in science or math. This is nonsense! Girls are just as capable as boys. In addition, once they reach high school, even teachers and other adults may give girls the indirect and subtle message that they are less likely to succeed in math or science than boys are. While some schools are working hard to rectify this problem, it does still exist.

So, try to be sure that your daughter does not eliminate a possible career choice simply because of assumptions she has made based only on being female. What is most important is not that you convince your daughter to enter any particular career, but that you give your daughter the message that gender does not determine an individual's skills or talents and should not determine her career choice either.

How can we encourage adolescent girls to strive more academically and less socially?
Shivana N.

Adolescent girls seem to *need* more social time than adolescent boys. From a very early age, girls are taught to pay more attention to the needs and feelings of others than boys are. Boys are encouraged to "build towers," compete, and show their strength, whereas young girls are rewarded for being caring, sensitive, and helpful to others. So, it really should come as no surprise that adolescent girls are more "socially driven" than adolescent boys. And as a result, it is particularly difficult for a teen girl when she is left out or rejected.

In addition to strong social needs, there are two other reasons why your daughter may not be putting an appropriate amount of effort and attention into her schoolwork.

- First, like many adolescents, your daughter may have a problem with time management. She may not be deliberately neglecting her schoolwork; she simply may not know how to manage her time in order to balance academics with her social life.

Learning how to balance a social life and school-work is not easy.

- Second, your daughter may not see or be able to focus on the long-term implications of not putting more effort into her schoolwork. If her social life feels far more important and satisfying to her at the moment, she may neglect or actively resist doing her schoolwork. It is normal for teens to focus primarily on the here and now. The idea that their high school grades could affect them far into the future is sometimes hard for them to take seriously.

Here are some tips for helping your daughter to achieve a reasonable balance between schoolwork and her social life:

- Start with the *expectation* that she will try her best. Your belief in her abilities lays the foundation for her belief in herself. As her parent, it is very important that you *do* have high expectations for your daughter, so she will feel loved, cared about, and encouraged to achieve.
- Maintain an ongoing dialogue with your daughter about how she is doing in school. Don't just pay attention to your daughter's schoolwork when she gets a poor grade on her report card or fails an exam. Showing your interest *all* of the time is a reflection of your belief that her academics are important to her future.
- Ask your daughter to share papers or essays she has written, *not* for your criticism but as a way of

learning more about the things she is studying in school.

- Actively communicate to your daughter that her schoolwork is very important and be prepared, if necessary, to set limits on and curtail her time for socializing.

- Consider making certain privileges, like getting her driver's license or extending her curfew, dependent on the *effort* she puts into her schoolwork. Look for teacher comments on her report card about how hard she has been trying. Remember that not all kids are "A" students. It is OK to get a "C" if that is truly her best effort.

* * *

Girls who have a history of having to struggle to get by in school often stop striving academically and put all of their time and energy into their social life once they reach their teen years. In middle school or high school, when the academic demands increase, they become so frustrated that they simply "give up." If your daughter has had too much damage to her self-esteem as a learner, no matter what you do at this point, or how many limits you set, there's probably not much more that you alone can do. Things have likely reached a point where you need outside assistance in determining what the problem is and how you can get your daughter the help she needs.

Don't fall into the trap of blaming your daughter. It won't help and it will only alienate her from you more. Instead find out what the problem is, what help your daughter needs, and how you are going to make sure she gets it. This means that she needs you to become her advocate, not her enemy.

- Start by contacting your daughter's doctor and school counselor. Tell them that you want a referral to the school psychologist or other expert so that your daughter can be tested to see what, if any, learning disabilities or special learning needs she may have.
- Meet with her teachers to see what they are doing to help her succeed in the classroom. Find out if they are available for extra help or if the school provides any kind of tutoring service.
- Find out about special programs that might be available to help your daughter. Some schools run "alternative education" programs, or there might be opportunities for more hands-on learning through occupational education programs or community internships.
- If your daughter's school does not have the resources to help, contact your State Education Department to learn about your daughter's rights as a student and the school district's responsibilities to provide her with an appropriate educational program.
- No matter what, if you don't want your daughter to give up on herself, don't give up on her!

If your daughter sees that you are on her side, and that you are doing everything you can to help her, then she will more likely do everything *she* can. Don't expect a sudden turnaround—it's a slow process that will require your ongoing attention. Your goal is to build your daughter's self-esteem as a learner and to teach her to appropriately advocate for her own needs.

As a parent, should I speak openly about my own adolescent experiences, good and bad, as examples of where I have been and how my choices and experiences have impacted where I am today? *Ann M.*

Yes, yes, yes! You have 30, 40, maybe even 50 years of experiences under your belt at this point. Why hide what you have learned from your daughter? And more importantly, if you made mistakes (and we all have), sharing them with your daughter makes you much more believable and human. Nobody likes living with, or listening to, someone who presents themselves as perfect and acts as if they "walk on water."

But there is a tricky part to being open about your adolescent experiences—and this has to do with timing. You need to carefully consider *what* you tell your daughter and *when* you tell her.

Deciding *when* to tell her something about your past mistakes (or errors in judgment) should have less to do with your daughter's chronological age and more to do with her emotional maturity. If you give her personal information that she is not ready to hear, she may ignore it (if you're lucky), she may misinterpret it to mean that you are encouraging her or giving her permission to do what you did, or she may gossip with friends about it, and you could find your personal history being repeated on the phone, or on-line!

In deciding *what* to tell your daughter, think about what important "lesson" you learned from a particular experience, and whether or not this is a lesson that would be valuable to her at this point in her life. Being open and honest with your daughter will foster a closer connection and encourage her to be open and honest with you.

* * *

Sharing your adolescent experiences with your daughter can be lots of fun, in addition to helping her understand how you got to be who you are and where you are today. Teens love to hear juicy stories about things their parents did when they were teenagers—particularly when parents are not using their experiences to teach their kids a lesson! So try to let your daughter in on some of where you've been, just in the course of conversation, like when you're driving to an appointment or having breakfast together. It can also be a wonderful bonding experience to get together with some of your daughter's friends and their parents to talk about "the good old days"—which may not have always been so good. In this way, you can share with your daughter the wealth of experiences of many parents, not just your own. Remember, not all of these conversations have to be serious and heavy. You can be humorous and light-hearted and have a great time together.

How can I impress on my daughter the importance of decisions made now and how these decisions will influence her life in the future? *Melissa K.*

As a parent, your natural instinct is to try to steer your daughter in the "right" direction. You want to keep her from experiencing failures, hurts, and mistakes. However, it is important not to get involved in *all* of your daughter's decisions. Some decisions she must make now will affect her far into the future, and therefore your input is probably very important. There are many other decisions that are *not* critically important. For those, your role is clear: Stay out of them!

The earlier your daughter starts to learn how to make her own decisions, even small ones, the better she will be at making more important decisions later on. For example, if a 10-year-old wants to go outside without her jacket, and her mother argues with her and tells her that she will be too cold and must put one on, the daughter will have been prevented from discovering for herself that she would prefer to wear a jacket when it is cold out. If you constantly anticipate and interfere with your daughter's making her own choices, you rob her of the opportunity to discover the consequences or outcomes of her own decisions.

If you have been intervening too much and have not given your daughter the opportunity to learn from making at least some of her own decisions, all is not lost. You can start now by making a conscious decision to back off. In doing so, you must remember that initially, your daughter will not be very good at decision making. In fact, some of her early choices are likely to be *poor* ones. Let this happen (unless, of course, the decision has important lifelong consequences). Learning to make good decisions comes with experience, so be patient.

Let's consider a typical decision-making opportunity in which you might be tempted to get involved. Your daughter is at the shoe store and sees a pair of shoes she is "dying" to have. When she tries them on and walks in them, you can see that they will be uncomfortable and impractical. But, even when you ask her if they fit well, she insists that they are perfect—clearly because she has her heart set on them. What do you do? Do you tell her she can't buy them? Do you tell her it's obvious that they don't fit quite right? Do you have a screaming match in the store? Or do you just wonder aloud how uncomfortable they seem—but then allow her to make the final decision by herself (silently acknowledging that she's is going to try to get you to buy another pair of shoes once she finally realizes that she made a poor decision)? The last option is by far the best! Let her make her own decision; let her live with the consequences. Be supportive, and don't be punitive or communicate an unspoken "I told you so!" (And, of course, don't give in to buying another pair of shoes when her decision backfires!) Experiences like these are the only way your daughter can begin to learn how decisions made today will influence her life in the future.

* * *

The backdrop for learning how to make good decisions is learning how your behavior affects your life. So, if you want your daughter to build the right foundation, start paying attention to the numerous opportunities you have now to help her learn how each of her choices and decisions has consequences. For example, if you constantly remind your daughter to remember her lunch money, or if you drop it off at school when she forgets it, she certainly isn't going to focus on the connection between remembering to take her lunch money in the morning and being able to buy food when she is starving at lunchtime. So, if she leaves her lunch money home, let her figure out how to handle it. She may borrow money from a friend, get someone to split their lunch with her, or even go hungry. None of these consequences are life threatening or lifelong. In the same way, while it's OK to *occasionally* wake your daughter up if she has slept through her alarm, it's not your job to stand by her bed *each and every* morning to get her up. And, if she does not make it to school or gets there late, don't give her a note excusing her. Let her deal with the consequences. While you must intervene in anything that is or could become a life-threatening situation (like physical safety), most other situations in which you are tempted to intervene probably reflect your own discomfort in allowing your daughter to "suffer."

The earlier in your daughter's life that you allow her to learn about the connections between certain behaviors and their outcomes, the better prepared she will be to make more important decisions later on, such as to keep or drop a class; to continue with or drop out of a sport or other activity; to stay with one group of friends or move on to another; to put off her homework until it's too late to get it done or to start it early; to drink or not drink alcohol at a party; or even whether or not to experiment with drugs. The process of figuring out how decisions that she makes now will influence her in the future begins early on. Your job is to slowly but surely hand over more and more of the decision making to your daughter, so that by the time she leaves home, both you and she are confident in her ability to make good decisions that will positively influence her life.

How can I get my daughter to understand money? In these times, we need to raise our daughters to be self-sufficient. *Blair Y.*

Your daughter can best learn how to handle money through a combination of the example that you set for her and her own personal experiences.

First, in terms of the example that you set, as with

so many other things, your daughter will learn more from what you do than what you say. Be a good role model for financial responsibility. And, if you share your financial responsibilities with a spouse or other partner, remember that how you model shared money management will have a very significant impact on your daughter. Here are some of the questions you can ask yourself about what you do (or don't do) to set an example for your daughter:

- Do you live from paycheck to paycheck, or do you at least save something every week or every month?
- Are you an impulse buyer or are your purchases well planned and thoughtful?
- Do you argue with your spouse or partner about money, or do you have ongoing conversations about how the finances are handled?
- When you make a financial mistake, do you admit your error and discuss it openly so she can learn from your experience?
- Do you use credit cards in a responsible way?
- Do you have a budget? And do you live by it?

Second, in terms of your daughter's own personal experiences, she needs to learn by doing. Some of the lessons may be difficult, but it is better for her to make small mistakes now than big ones later on. Since your daughter is not likely to learn money management skills in school, it is really up to you to be her teacher and mentor. Start early, and build her financial understanding and self-esteem as a good money-manager.

* * *

Ironically, parents are as unlikely to talk with their daughters about money as they are about sex! It is, however, critical that you teach your daughter how to deal with money and finances. To help you, here are few tips that focus on preparing your daughter to eventually become financially self-sufficient. The tips begin with those that are appropriate for younger teens and take you through steps of increasing financial responsibility.

- Give your daughter a weekly allowance. Decide in advance what expenses she will be responsible for, like her own entertainment and special purchases, and help her work out a budget. Let her learn first-hand that when she spends too much and runs out of money, she'll have to wait until the following week for her next "paycheck."
- As soon as she is old enough to help out at home, provide your daughter with opportunities to earn money. Pay her a "salary" for doing special chores or particular jobs around the house.
- Insist that your daughter save a certain fixed amount or percentage of her "income" each week. This will help her learn the benefits of saving her money for the more expensive things she wants. It will also help her to build a cash reserve in case

she suddenly wants to make an unplanned purchase, like a great sweater that just went on sale.

- Set up a savings account and be sure your daughter understands the monthly bank statements. Explain to her how the interest she earns, and the regular deposits she makes, help her savings to grow.

- As she gets older, help your daughter to pick a special financial goal, like saving money for concert tickets or a new outfit, and work with her to monitor her progress in that direction.

- When she is old enough, encourage your daughter to find a part-time job. Jobs don't only mean working at a store or movie theater but include work like babysitting, mowing lawns, shoveling snow, or delivering newspapers.

- Once she is earning a reasonable amount of money, it is time for your daughter to have a checking account with ATM access. You might even put a small amount of money in her account for starters, but let *her* manage the account. Be sure to show her how to write and record checks and how to balance a bank statement each month.

- Explain to your daughter how you budget your money to pay bills, use credit cards responsibly, and save for retirement. Show her the downfalls of paying interest on debts. Once she understands the basics, talk with her about mortgages, buying things over time, and how to "shop" for the best credit. Talk with her about the choices you make concerning how you budget and spend money.

- Teach your daughter about investing her money, including how the stock market works, and how to find out about other investment opportunities. If this is not your area of expertise, or if you never learned about investing, there are more and more free seminars where she can go (and why don't you join her?) to learn about stocks, bonds, mutual funds, and so on.

- Finally, if your daughter has to file a tax return, don't do it for her. Instead, sit down with her and go through the process together. If you use an accountant, bring your daughter along. While initially much of the information may go over her head, she will at least begin to absorb the knowledge she will need for when she has to do this all on her own.

* * *

People's *values* are partially reflected in how they spend their money. If your daughter has learned that possessions are most important, and that she must have the "right" clothing, shoes, car, and so on, this is how she will measure her worth as a person. Clearly, her priorities will wind up in the wrong place. Your daughter needs to learn the value of using her money not only for her own material needs and wants but also as a way to reach out and help others. Have you talked with your daughter about donating at least some of her money to charity? You might tell her about the different charities and causes that you give money to, and how you made those decisions. Emphasize how good this kind of giving makes you feel!

I've become doubtful about steady continuing progress toward women's freedom and equality. Am I raising my daughter's hopes, only for her to come up against the same old glass ceiling? *Madeline V.*

As you know, the *glass ceiling* is the phrase that has come to represent the almost invisible limitations that many women encounter in the workplace when they try to rise to high-level positions. False assumptions, such as the idea that men should lead and women should follow, or that a woman's place is in the home, or that once a woman gets pregnant she should or will quit her job, or that men are smarter than women, have all become barriers that have prevented women from being promoted to top-level supervisory and management positions. It is because these false assumptions arise from centuries of living in a dominant male culture that it has been very difficult for women to not only convince men that they are equal, but often to convince themselves. These underlying assumptions have made the barriers "invisible"; therefore they are extremely hard to identify, confront, and overcome.

While the glass ceiling has not disappeared, it is certainly higher than ever before. Sadly, it is still true that, on average, women are paid less than men for the same work, and continue to be discriminated against being promoted to top positions, such as company president or CEO. However, more women than ever now hold high-level managerial and executive positions, and an even greater percentage are in middle management. So, depending on her career choice, your daughter might well come up against a glass ceiling. The good news is that it is not the "same old glass ceiling"—it is a higher one! The bad news is that there still is a glass ceiling at all.

The fact that a glass ceiling still exists does not mean you are giving your daughter false hopes by encouraging her to believe that she can achieve equality with men in the workplace. But in order to do this, she must *believe* that she is entitled to equality and she must learn to stand up and give voice to injustices. Let your daughter know that you believe that she can meet the challenge. But, be careful that in your desire to support her goals, you do not give her the idea that working to raise a glass ceiling is the path that she is "supposed" to take.

Support your daughter in finding her own way and in discovering what she wants in her life. Tell your daughter about the challenges she may face in regard to gender inequalities in the workplace. Unless you raise your daughter's consciousness about these issues, she might easily come to assume, as many women have, that there is just no place for her "at the top."

* * *

While the term *glass ceiling* has come to define gender inequalities in the workplace, an equally important and far more prevalent gender inequality remains in the "homeplace." There is greater gender inequality in who runs the household than there is in almost any American business. The vast majority of women who work full time outside of the home continue to work full time inside the home. They maintain the major responsibility for both raising the children and running the household. The vast majority of working American women, with or without children, hold the equivalent of two full-time jobs.

If your own family reflects this kind of traditional gender inequality, your daughter is more likely to grow up believing that it is simply "her job" to take care of the children and run the household, along with trying to manage her career. However, even if your family does tend to run on traditional tracks, you can help your daughter to see that she has other choices.

Talk with your daughter about how you might have done things very differently if you had been more conscious of these issues earlier on. Emphasize to her that while it may be very difficult to not repeat the patterns she saw in her own family, she *can* do it differently. Help your daughter to recognize how important it is to choose a life partner who is also committed to gender equality in the homeplace. It is particularly important for your daughter to hear from men who support and respect gender equality in the home. Then, she will more likely have the strength and resiliency to fight the "homeplace glass ceiling."

Be sure to communicate that equality in the homeplace is not a privilege only for women who work outside the home. Often, running a household takes more time and energy than any paying full-time job. Let your daughter know that choosing to remain at home to raise children is not an easier or "lesser" choice than working outside of the home. The greatest gift you can give your daughter is the confidence and competence that will allow her to choose her own path, and to change her mind if she wants to.

What have been girls'/women's gains and losses since the onset of the feminist movement? *Jessica B.*

You are right: There have been both gains and losses as a result of the feminist movement. In addition, what one person might consider a gain or a loss may be quite different from another person. In general, those people with a feminist perspective often identify the following as the major gains and losses.

Gains

- More career opportunities and choices.
- More sports and athletic opportunities and choices.

- More lifestyle choices—"settling down" to marriage with children isn't the only acceptable goal.
- More freedom to express one's gender orientation, whether it be heterosexual, homosexual, or bisexual.
- More sexual freedom in general.
- More birth control options.
- More choices about a woman's own body, including the option of abortion if she has an unwanted pregnancy.
- More focus and research on the health issues that are specific to women, such as breast cancer.

Losses

- Femininity is often seen as sexist and not OK.
- Gallantry is often seen as sexist and not OK.
- Health risks for women are becoming more similar to those of men (like heart disease and high blood pressure) as their role distinctions diminish.
- Career pressures have been added to the traditional responsibilities of maintaining the household, motherhood, and caring for the older generation, so many women work full time and then have a second full-time job at home.
- Stress and the pressure to be a "superwoman" are rampant.
- Eating disorders are rampant.
- Depression and anxiety disorders are on the rise.

The fact that there have been both gains and losses certainly does not suggest that the feminist movement has not been a good thing for both men and women. Whenever new opportunities are created, there are inevitably some losses.

How can I encourage my daughter to look at the future, when she is only looking at today? *Denise F.*

Before you get too distressed or discouraged about your daughter's perspective of "only looking at today," try to remember your own teen years. Can you remember the days when your "future" was summer vacation, or who your teacher was going to be next year, or when you would start high school, have permission to date, or be old enough to drive? Try to reflect back on your adolescence and remember what you were focused on. Is your daughter really any different? It is normal for your daughter to be focused on the here and now, or on the "immediate future," rather than on long-range plans. It's a typical adolescent perspective.

Of course, in spite of this truth, it is important to encourage your daughter to keep her future in mind. You can do this by asking her questions, like "What do you think will happen if you . . . ?" or "Have you considered the possibility of . . . ?" Questions that encourage your daughter to make connections between today and tomorrow are a great way to

get her to look at the future and not be totally ab-
sorbed in the present.

But don't expect too much. Adolescents are no-
toriously stuck in the here and now. Actually, they
often know how to relish the here and now—something that many adults should learn how to do!

* * *

One of the best ways to motivate your daughter
to think ahead and prepare for her future is to get
her excited about the possibilities of different careers,
and the lifestyles associated with them. Here are some
specific things you can do:

- Let your daughter know that you believe that she
  can be almost anything she wants to be.
- Give her the opportunity to meet people from diverse careers and walks of life. One of the best ways
  to do this is to ask friends and family to tell her
  about what they do, how they like it, and how they
  got there.
- Give her information about different opportunities
  and career paths. There are plenty of books and
  new magazines that focus on women and work. As
  she gets older, talk with her more about the realities of different jobs and careers: those that are on
  the upswing, those that look like they provide the
  greatest security, typical starting salaries, and so on.
- Encourage and support her in exploring and developing her skills and talents. Remember that this

is a time to try many new things, not to feel like she's got to stick with the same thing for years.

■ Help your daughter think about the costs and expenses of certain lifestyles and how she needs to consider how much money she wants to earn, as well as what she would like to do.

But remember—it's your daughter's life, not yours. So be careful not to impose your choices and desires on her. Your job is to help her explore the options and see many different careers "in action."

What are the anticipated needs of this generation of adolescent girls as they make the transition to young adulthood?
Sarah M.

There are three major "needs" that are likely to be important for your daughter's positive transition to adulthood.

First, it is important to teach your daughter about her own health and encourage her to actively seek answers and opinions about health-related issues.

■ She needs to "take charge" of her health through good prevention and health maintenance strategies, including a healthy diet and regular exercise, monthly breast self-examinations, yearly Pap smears, and regular checkups with her physician.

■ She needs to know and understand the dangers of eating disorders—and how they can actually do long-term damage or even be deadly.

- She needs to be well informed about STDs, pregnancy, and effective contraception.

As a parent, it is your responsibility to make sure that your daughter has access to the most accurate and up-to-date health information possible. Be aware, too, that some of the information that she might obtain on the Internet, or from friends or other sources, could be inaccurate, misleading, or even wrong and harmful. If you are not sure where to get the most recent and accurate information, talk to your daughter's doctor, school nurse, or even the local librarian.

Second, familiarity with the new technologies is no longer an option. It is a necessity. Your daughter's adulthood is likely to be vastly different from yours in terms of the prevalence of technology in *all* aspects of her life. And, while men still dominate the technological fields, women must understand the importance of becoming equal contributors, partners, and consumers of technology—or they will be left behind. Therefore, you need to ensure that your daughter has ongoing access to the new technologies through her school, your local library, and if possible, at home.

Third, your daughter must be prepared to take care of herself. She needs to be self-reliant and self-sufficient and not assume that she will have a partner to take care of her. In fact, the present trend suggests that more and more women are deciding to put off marriage until they have finished their education and begun their careers. In addition, many women today feel comfortable deciding not to marry at all. Even if they do marry, the high divorce rate makes it increasingly important that they have the skills and strategies necessary for self-reliance. Your daughter needs to be confident enough to take charge of her own life and not be dependent on anyone else to run her life for her. Teach her that being self-sufficient does not mean that she limits her relationship choices but rather that she is far less likely to feel trapped and stay in a relationship just because she can't take care of herself.

* * *

Although women's specific needs certainly change from generation to generation, and we can't always predict exactly what the next generation will need, what we do know is that the more we teach our daughters to believe in themselves, the better prepared they will be for the challenges ahead. Today's young women have opportunities open to them as never before. As they pursue these opportunities, it is important that they do so as women of integrity and not compromise their integrity for money or convenience.

Young women today need role models who have demonstrated their integrity through the courage to hold true to their convictions, even though they may be unpopular. They need role models who follow through with their commitments and keep their promises. They need role models who listen to their own voices and are not swayed by the need for approval. They need role models who encourage and build women up, rather than to tear them down with slanderous talk, criticism, and gossip.

As you pass this world to your daughter and her generation, you need to equip her with these tools of integrity, morality, courage, and love. Certainly one of the best ways to do this is through the example you set for her.

Hot Tips

☞ It's a fact that most adolescent girls need more time for socialization than adolescent boys do. If your daughter's socializing is significantly interfering with her schoolwork or responsibilities, she may have a problem with time management. If this is the problem, you need to step in and set appropriate limits on her socialization. At the same time, your daughter needs help learning how to manage her time. Give her specific and manageable goals that she must reach to get you off her back. And when she does, you should relax the limits and give her another chance to manage more independently.

☞ If your daughter seems to be struggling with schoolwork, or if she begins to get consistently poor grades in spite of what appear to be reasonable efforts on her part, she may have a learning problem. Before you come down hard on her, get an educational evaluation through her school. You want to be sure that your daughter does not have a learning disability or other problem that is causing her poor performance. Do not assume that your daughter is simply not spending enough time on her schoolwork. After all, most of us will stop trying to do something if we keep failing.

☞ There is no question that sharing your own adolescent experiences with your daughter can be extremely helpful for her and can bring you closer together. The part you have to watch out for is your timing. *What* you tell your daughter and *when* you tell her depend on her level of maturity. Ask yourself if what you are thinking about sharing with your daughter will be helpful to her at this time in her life. If your answer is yes, then go ahead. Otherwise wait. There is plenty of time.

☞ While you may want to be sure that your daughter makes all the right choices now, if you make all of her decisions for her, it will hurt her rather than help her. Of course, there are some decisions that have such important consequences that you shouldn't allow your daughter to have control over them. But, whenever possible, give your daughter the opportunity to make her own decisions. She needs to see what happens as a result of her choices so she can learn from her own experience.

☞ Your daughter will learn how to manage money

in two ways: first, by seeing how you do, or don't, manage your money; and, second, by having increasing responsibility for managing her own money and expenses. Start with a weekly allowance, from which your daughter must pay for certain things, and gradually move toward her having total control over her own bank accounts, including a checking account, savings account, and ATM card.

☞ While you might have your own ideas about what career your daughter should choose, remember, it is *her* life. Encourage her to consider the vast number of choices she has, including possibilities in more traditionally "male" careers, like the fields of math or science. As she gets older, help your daughter to investigate the realities of different career choices, like educational requirements, pay, mobility, and so on.

☞ While women have yet to achieve full equality in the workplace, things have improved. The glass ceiling is rising and your daughter can be part of it rising even higher. While your daughter needs to be conscious of workplace discrimination, don't encourage her to stay away from a career or the pursuit of a promotion just because she is a woman. Encourage her to fight for her equal rights!

☞ While some see the feminist movement as benefiting only women, particularly in the workplace, it can be helpful to point out to your daughter how it has also benefited men. Men have gained increased "permission" to express their feelings, greater recognition of the importance of their role as fathers to their children, and partnership with women in earning money to support the family.

☞ As your daughter moves into adulthood, she needs to be prepared to take on the responsibilities for her physical, emotional, and financial health. This means that she needs you, as her parent, to help her learn how to take care of herself and find resources in each of these arenas. Your daughter needs to know how to use the "new technologies," which will increasingly be the source of the information she will need to continue to take care of herself.

☞ It is part of the nature of adolescence for your daughter to be focused primarily on the here and now. While your daughter needs to become increasingly attentive to planning for her future, she is not yet an adult. Don't forget to give her room to enjoy her teen years.

And

The Final Hot Tip

Enjoy your daughter's teen years.
They will be gone before you know it.
Take every opportunity to share
in this glorious time of her life!

Personal Notes and Thoughts

Personal Notes and Thoughts